LIVING YOUR DASH

HOW TO FIND AND FULFILL
YOUR LIFE PURPOSE

RICK HALE

Karen,

Live everyday of your "Dash" for God.

[signature]

Nehemiah 8:10

GENESIS PUBLISHING COMPANY
Roswell, New Mexico

PUBLISHED BY
GENESIS PUBLISHING COMPANY
Roswell, New Mexico

ISBN 978-0-9916291-5-2

Printed in the United States of America

January 2016
First Edition

DEDICATION

This book is dedicated to my wife, Mary.
Thanks for saying, "I do!" in a moment of insanity.
It has been a wonderful adventure living our dash together.

CONTENTS

P R E F A C E

There comes a special moment in everyone's life,
a moment for which that person was born. That special
opportunity, when he seizes it, will fulfill his mission —
a mission for which he is uniquely qualified. In that moment,
he finds greatness. It is his finest hour.
Winston Churchill

What if Winston Churchill is correct? What if there really is a special moment and a unique mission for everyone, without exception? If this is true, then finding and fulfilling this life mission is of utmost importance for all people. Otherwise, people could live an entire lifetime, yet miss their reason for being on the planet.

This book is about finding and fulfilling your life purpose. You are not here by accident; you are not the accidental result of a cosmic explosion. There is more to your life than simply taking up space and breathing up all the good air. You have been placed here by God for a reason and you alone are uniquely qualified and equipped to discover and accomplish your reason for being.

I have conducted several hundred funerals in my years of pastoral ministry. I still find it to be a travesty, bordering on obscenity, when people come to the end of their lives, but have never discovered their reason for being here. What a disappointment when people live 60, 70 or 80 years, look in the rear-view mirror and say, "What was that all about?" What a rewarding contrast it is when I have the privilege of conducting the funeral services for people who have truly lived out their God-given life mission. Friends and family leave these services with a sense of joy and satisfaction, knowing that their loved one's life was not lived in vain.

I wish I could have conducted the funeral service for Nehemiah. Talk about a guy who successfully discovered his unique mission and then lived it. This relatively unknown Old Testament character shines as a magnificent example of what it takes to seize and fulfill a life mission. Few have discovered the life-changing message contained in the pages of this man's book. Somehow the impact of Nehemiah's story has failed to influence the way we live our lives.

The Book of Nehemiah is not so much a book as it is a journal. Much of Nehemiah's story is told autobiographically, giving us the rare opportunity of looking over his shoulder as he takes pen in hand and makes entries into his personal journal.

Nehemiah's particular style of writing affords us the unique perspective of watching his life mission unfold before our eyes. But more than that, it allows us to learn what it takes for a person to successfully find and fulfill a life mission. Instead of a didactic lecture, Nehemiah fleshes out before us the real life story of a person in passionate pursuit of his reason for being. He invites us into his journey so that we can see the good, the bad and the ugly of fulfilling God's purpose. Nehemiah tells it like it is. He allows us to experience the highs and lows of a life on mission for God.

Nehemiah is a man for all seasons. His story can be our story, but we must be willing to learn from his example and have the courage to follow in his footsteps. The journey will be difficult at times, but the rewards are worth the costs for the person willing to say yes to God's invitation to the journey.

I intentionally tell most of Nehemiah's story in the present tense. Even though the events of his life happened almost 2,500 years ago, I want you to feel like you are living in Jerusalem with Nehemiah, transported back in time to 444 B.C. so that you can experience the adventure as it unfolds in Nehemiah's journal.

I want you to read these pages as if Nehemiah is speaking directly to you. Because of this, you can expect to see the word *you* often. We are reading a man's journal and most people keep their journals private. I am convinced Nehemiah makes his journal public for one reason: *you*. Nehemiah publishes his journal because its message is about you and for you. Nehemiah wants to share with others the life-transforming lessons he has learned. This may even be the reason God has chosen to include Nehemiah's journal in the canon of Scripture.

You will be disappointed if you are hoping this will be another commentary on The Book of Nehemiah. There have been some wonderful books written over the years about Nehemiah. Some focus on critical issues while others focus on principles of leadership. This is neither a commentary nor a leadership book.

This book is for people on a quest to discover their reason for being. It is designed to be a practical guidebook to help people discover their unique purpose in life and to offer proven steps to achieve this purpose. In his letter to the Ephesians, the Apostle Paul writes, *"For we are God's workmanship, created in Christ Jesus to do good works, which God prepared in advance for us to do"* (Ephesians 2:10). What are the good works God has prepared in advance for you to do? More specifically, is there one special mission he has written below your name?

Think of this book as a road trip we will take together. It is a journey toward the destination of discovering our reason for being on this planet. This is what we will call our life mission or life purpose. Our goal is to use Nehemiah's journal as our roadmap for the trip, allowing it to guide us through the ups and downs on our adventure to finding and fulfilling our life mission.

I offer a special thank you to Dr. Lendell Nolan and Nelda Massey for creating the Personal Application questions sprinkled throughout the book and the Action Steps at the conclusion of each chapter. I encourage you to use these tools to apply and personalize your own life mission. I am deeply indebted to Jane Anglin and Jerry Holm for contributing their editing and proof-reading skills to this project.

Winston Churchill was correct. There really is a special moment for which everyone was born, a special mission for which everyone is uniquely qualified. We just have to find it. And when we do, we will find greatness. We will discover our finest hour.

Thank you for taking this journey into the life of Nehemiah. My prayer is that the story of his life mission will inspire you to find and fulfill your life purpose. This is what living your dash is all about. But what does it mean to *live your dash?* Read on and you will see. Let the adventure begin!

LIVING YOUR DASH

C all me crazy. Call me superstitious. But don't call me to ride in a hearse.

I have been a pastor for over 35 years, so I have done my share of funerals. But I have never enjoyed riding in the hearse to the cemetery. When I conduct a memorial service, the funeral home directors nearly always invite me to ride with them in the hearse from the funeral home to the graveside service, but I usually decline their offer. I don't know what bothers me most about riding in a hearse. Perhaps it's being in such close proximity to a dead body or riding with a person who handles dead bodies for a living (I seem to remember something in the Old Testament about this kind of activity making a person ceremonially unclean). Maybe what bothers me is driving ten miles an hour in a funeral processional to the cemetery. I drive faster than that in my garage. At any rate, I generally drive my own car to the cemetery.

The end result of this decision to solo to the cemetery is that I arrive long before the funeral procession arrives. Since there are not many activities a person can do while waiting at a cemetery, I spend my time looking at gravestones. You can learn a lot about people by looking at their gravestones. Gravestones come in all shapes and sizes. Some are ornate, others are simple. Some are large and expensive, others are small and cheap. Some are old and weathered while others are sitting at the head of freshly turned soil. Some have beautiful tributes inscribed in stone giving testimony to the person buried beneath. Others simply offer a name, followed by the date of birth and the date of death.

One day as I waited for the funeral procession to arrive, it dawned on me that in the midst of all the variety represented on the grave markers, there was one common denominator shared by every single headstone. It was the dash. Between the date of birth and the date of death there was a dash on every gravestone. As I focused in on one particular dash, I suddenly realized how that short line represented something of great significance. It was a symbol of the deceased person's entire life. Everything that happened in that person's life – from the day he exited his mother's womb to the day he entered eternity – was represented in that single dash.

There I stood in the cemetery, surrounded by thousands of gravestones with thousands of dashes. I began to wonder how these people, unknown to me, had lived their dashes. Were their dashes filled with meaning and purpose? Did they live their dashes serving others or serving themselves? What would their friends and family say about the value of their individual friend's dash? Did their dashes leave a positive legacy on the planet, or did they waste their dashes?

As these questions churned in my mind, I saw the funeral processional begin to enter the cemetery. As I turned to prepare for the graveside service, I was struck with a fresh set of questions. These were personal questions. How am I living my dash? Have I lived my dash to this point in my life with meaning and purpose? How much of my dash is left? How much of my dash have I wasted? How will I live what's left of my dash? How would my family and friends honestly evaluate the way I am living my dash?

These are still to this day important questions for me to answer because I know that someday in the not-so-distant future I will be forced to ride to the cemetery in the hearse. But this time, it will not be in the front seat with the funeral home director. This time I will be in the back, in a wooden box, leading the funeral processional at ten miles an hour. On that day, my dash will be complete.

This book is all about living our dashes, or at least, what is left of them. We cannot go back in time to redo or undo what has already been done. But we do have today, and perhaps tomorrow. What will we do with the time we have left?

In describing the dash, I like to use the terms *life purpose* and *life mission*. I am convinced more now than ever before that God has a mission for every person on this planet. We are not here by accident. We are created for a purpose; we are made for a mission. It is one thing to believe we are made for a purpose in life, but it is something quite different to actually find and fulfill this life purpose.

How can we find our life purpose, and once we find it, how can we fulfill it? One way is to find other people who have already done it well and learn from their experience. We need to find people who have successfully lived their dashes and created a legacy that honors God.

I have found such a person. Even though his story is found in the pages of Scripture, many people have never taken a long look at his life. Maybe people have "ho-hummed" his life because of the nature of his life purpose. The guy's God-given mission in life was to build a wall. See what I mean? You may have just been tempted to yawn. Not very exciting as life purposes go. But obviously God found his story exciting and important enough to include it in the Bible. In fact, an entire book in the Bible bears his name and tells his story. How many people can make this claim about their life purpose?

The year is 444 B.C. Nehemiah is a Jew living in Persia where he serves as the cupbearer to King Artaxerxes. The Jewish capital city of Jerusalem had been destroyed 143 years earlier in 587 B.C. by the Babylonians. Some Jews had returned to re-inhabit Jerusalem during the century before Nehemiah's day. But now Nehemiah learns the inhabitants of Jerusalem are in great distress. One of the primary reasons for their distress is they are living in a wall-less city. There is no wall around Jerusalem to protect the inhabitants from their enemies.

The Book of Nehemiah tells the story of how Nehemiah built a wall around Jerusalem. However, you must understand this is much more than just a construction story. This is a story of a man finding and fulfilling his God-given, God-ordained life purpose. From his example, we hope to do the same.

In my years of pastoral ministry, I have seen my share of tragedies and heartaches. But none rivals the sadness I feel when I see people live their entire lives and never discover their life purpose. What a horrible scene, to witness a life lived without purpose, direction or meaning. To see a wasted life has become painful for me. There is no legitimate excuse for this to happen, yet we see it occurring around us every day. But here is the good news. Our experience can be different. We don't have to waste our dashes. From the example of a simple Jewish cupbearer, we can learn the steps needed to find and fulfill our life purpose.

You may think what I am describing is impossible in your life because you have made too many wrong turns and bad decisions. But there is still hope for your dash if you are willing to take a chance on a new way of living. I always loved watching the old television show *Mission Impossible*. I especially enjoyed the opening scene every week. The leader of the Mission Impossible team would be given a secretly taped message, describing the details of the mission. The voice of the tape would always include one qualifier: *"Your mission, should you choose to accept it..."*

We are given the same qualifier with our life purpose. God has a mission for each of us, something he wants us to accomplish between today and our funeral. He is ready to reveal it, willing to inspire it, and able to empower it. But we have to be ready, willing, and able to pursue it.

Are you up for the challenge? Are you willing to take a chance at a new way of living? If not, close this book now and continue to live your dash without rhyme or reason. I hope you will take the challenge because I don't want you to be like the fellow who began each day with these words:

I get up each morning and dust off my wits,
Pick up the paper and read the obits.
If my name is missing, I know I'm not dead,
So I eat a good breakfast and go back to bed!

There is a better way to live the rest of your dash. It is the Nehemiah way. Take the challenge and you will discover God has a life purpose with your name on it. Your life purpose can truly be Mission Possible when God is involved. So get ready for the ride of your life as you find and fulfill your life purpose.

Here's the best part. Someday when you die, and you make that slow trip to the cemetery in the back of the hearse, the pastor won't have to make up stuff about you at the graveside. In fact, his greatest challenge will be deciding what he has to leave out.

Living Your Dash

At your funeral, what are two things that you would like a pastor or family member to be able to honestly say about you?

_____

_____

_____

_____

What are some of your short-term and long-term goals designed to help you become the person described above?

_____

_____

_____

_____

_____

_____

_____

_____

PART I

FINDING YOUR LIFE PURPOSE

THE TAKEOFF

Takeoffs can be tense times. Just look around at your fellow travelers the next time you fly the friendly skies. For some people, takeoffs create mild tension. For others, they are nothing short of terrifying. But for even the most seasoned traveler, the atmosphere in the cabin changes when the captain makes that final announcement, "Flight attendants, prepare the cabin for takeoff!" Seat belts are tightened, children are secured, armrests are gripped and prayers are prayed. Takeoffs can be tense times.

Life purpose takeoffs can also be tense times. Getting your life purpose airborne can seem like an impossible dream when parked at the end of the runway. Gigantic questions loom on the horizon: *What is God calling me to accomplish? How can I know my unique life purpose for certain? How do I start? Will this be a solo flight or will others be onboard to assist me? Will I encounter turbulence?* These are big questions; important questions; tension-causing questions.

Our friend Nehemiah faces the same questions as he attempts to get his life purpose off the ground. In the early chapters of his journal, Nehemiah takes us through a step by step process to help us get our life purpose airborne. One by one, he encounters and answers our questions.

Are you ready to begin the journey? Buckle up, secure the children and get a good grip on the armrest. Takeoffs can be tense times, but last time I checked, they are the only way to get airborne. By the end of part one of our journey, I hope to hear you shout, "Liftoff!"

Living Your Dash

What fears or anxieties do you have about finding and fulfilling your life purpose?

_____

_____

_____

_____

CATCH GOD'S VISION

Life is like a parachute jump; you've got to get it right the first time.

Eleanor Roosevelt

You only live once, but if you do it right, once is enough.

Mae West

On May 29, 1832 a man named Evariste Galois sat down and wrote a 60-page mathematical masterpiece in one sitting. Experts say he accomplished more in one night than most people accomplish in a lifetime. In his book, *Men of Mathematics*, Eric Bell writes, "What he wrote in those desperate long hours before dawn will keep generations of mathematicians busy for hundreds of years."

Why would Galois expend so much energy in writing his masterpiece in one sitting? There was a good reason. He had been challenged to a duel the day before. He knew this might be his last chance to leave his mathematical legacy. Galois treated May 29 as if it were the last day of his life. He wrote frantically and finished his work three hours before dawn. It was a good thing he completed the work. Galois died from gunshot wounds the next day. It had been the last day of his life.[1]

I am convinced God has a specific task for you to accomplish between now and your funeral. Let's call it your life purpose. What special project has God assigned to you? What specific undertaking has God penciled in next to your name? Like Evariste Galois, you cannot be sure how long you have left to accomplish your life purpose.

Granted, finding your mission in life is not an easy task. The problem for many people is not a lack of desire, but a lack of knowledge. Assembling the pieces of your life purpose can be as frustrating as putting together a puzzle when you are convinced a dog must have eaten some of the important pieces. This frustration can lead you to conclude that finding and fulfilling a life purpose must be a rare privilege reserved for the few. Perhaps you have been paralyzed with this feeling.

You know the names of famous people who have accomplished their life purpose.

Their names grace the pages of the history books: Abraham Lincoln led America through the Civil War; Winston Churchill guided England through World War II; Martin Luther King laid the foundation for the Civil Rights Movement; Walt Disney created family-friendly theme parks; Henry Ford perfected the assembly line method of producing affordable automobiles; Moses led the People of Israel out of Egyptian slavery. For these notable figures, their names are synonymous with their accomplished life purposes.

But what about people closer to home? The truth is, you know people who have either accomplished their life purpose or are successfully living it today. You can name friends and family who have raised a godly family, developed a God-honoring business, started a faith-based ministry, developed an effective non-profit organization, led an effective ministry, or coordinated a successful international mission project.

Who are some people you personally know who have caught God's vision for their lives?

_____

_____

_____

If the bull's-eye of a target was a 10 and the outer ring of the target a one, how on target are you in terms of finding and fulfilling God's purpose for your life?

_____

_____

_____

_____

_____

The Book of Nehemiah tells the story of a man named Nehemiah building a wall around the city of Jerusalem. But more importantly, it is the story of a man finding and fulfilling his life purpose. As noted earlier, the majority of the Book of Nehemiah reads like a journal. It is as if you are reading over his shoulder as he makes his daily journal entries. By reading his amazing story, you can learn from his personal experience how to find and fulfill your life purpose.

Where do you begin the process of finding your life purpose? You start where Nehemiah starts. You must first catch God's vision. You must be able to answer this question: "God, what do you want me to accomplish for you before my funeral? What project or task have you uniquely shaped me to complete?"

What does it take to catch God's vision for your life purpose? Nehemiah begins to answer that question in the first two chapters of his book. As you read through these early verses in Nehemiah's journal, listen carefully for the first steps in his journey to finding his life purpose.

Step #1 : Decide to Care
(Nehemiah 1:1-4)

One day Nehemiah receives a report from the inhabitants of Jerusalem and the news is not good. *"Those who survived the exile and are back in the province are in great trouble and disgrace. The wall of Jerusalem is broken down, and its gates have been burned with fire"* (v. 3). For Nehemiah, more than just a wall is broken. So is Nehemiah's heart. The distressing news is devastating to him. *"When I heard these things, I sat down and wept. For some days I mourned and fasted and prayed before the God of heaven"* (v. 4).

What touches your heart, stirs your emotions and moves you to tears? For Nehemiah, he cares about the Jewish exiles in distress in a city without walls. What do you care most about in life? This could be an important clue in finding your life purpose.

People don't all care about the same causes. This explains why you may have trouble getting everyone around you to get excited and passionate about the causes that touch your heart. What moves you to tears may move the next person to boredom and the causes that passionately move others do nothing to call you to action. This does not mean people are evil or uncaring. It simply reflects an important truth about the way God created people; God has uniquely shaped and fashioned each person's heart to fit a need in the world. If everyone cared about the same issues, many important needs would go unmet. This is God's creative way of insuring that the innumerable needs around the world are being met.

Does this help explain what is going on in your heart? There is a good reason why you are passionate about a certain cause. God has wired you that way. He has placed this passion within you as a motivator to inspire you to action. In fact, this is often the first indicator and piece of the puzzle in identifying your life purpose. Take a look at the world around you and ask yourself what touches your heart, stirs your emotions and moves you to tears?

Several years ago I heard the amazing story of Marie Emmanuelle. Marie is a Belgian nun who cares about hurting people. She had taught for 32 years at the Grand College of Istanbul, but at the age of 63 petitioned to be a missionary to one of the poorest places in the world – the Zabaline of Cairo. The Zabaline are the city's 40,000 garbage collectors. They collect garbage by day and live with their families at the city dumps. Forty percent of their children die in their first year from disease. Marie cares about these people and has made them her life purpose. She has already built a kindergarten, a dispensary, a dental clinic and a vocational school. She says, "These are the most beautiful years of my life."

Working at the city dump in Cairo may not be your calling in life, but it is Marie's. The critical question to ask is what arouses your heart's passions and emotions?

As a pastor, I love to see people in my church begin to catch God's vision for their lives. I have noticed over the years that the journey is often jump-started when people's hearts are touched by an unmet need in the community. Numerous ministries have been birthed in our town because people were moved with compassion. Our community has a regional food bank today because someone was concerned about hungry people. We have a recovery ministry because someone cared about people struggling with alcohol and drug abuse. There is a home for troubled teenagers because someone cared. Financial counseling is available free of charge because someone was concerned about people facing financial difficulties. Support groups for people struggling through divorce or grief are available because someone cared. Marriage mentoring is available for newlyweds because someone wants their marriages to succeed.

Compassion is a powerful motivator, especially for Christians. This should come as no surprise. Jesus was consistently moved with compassion when he witnessed hurting people. *"Jesus went through all the towns and villages, teaching in their synagogues, preaching the good news of the kingdom and healing every disease and sickness. When he saw the crowds, he had compassion on them, because they were harassed and helpless, like sheep without a shepherd. Then he said to his disciples, 'The harvest is plentiful but the workers are few. Ask the Lord of the harvest, therefore, to send out workers into his harvest field'"* (Matthew 9:35-38).

The Greek word for compassion used here is the word *splagchnon*. The word refers to the bowel or belly. In other words, when Jesus looked at the hurting and lost people in his world, he felt the agony in his gut. It was as if someone punched him in the stomach. It was his pain that motivated him to relieve their pain. Have you ever felt physical discomfort when you witnessed the painful circumstances of people around you?

We might expect Jesus to tell his disciples to pray for the harvest and to pray for these hurting people. However, he has a different challenge. Jesus tells his disciples to pray for more harvesters to go into the world to meet these needs. It is no surprise that this challenge at the end of Matthew nine is immediately followed in chapter 10 by Jesus sending his disciples on what scholars refer to as the limited commission. The goal of this short-term mission trip was to share the good news and extend a helping hand to hurting people.

What do you see in your world that causes you to feel this kind
needs around you that deeply touch your heart with this level of
the hurting people in your world in need of a healing touch? Th
come from your hands. Catching God's vision for your life purpos
cide to care.

> What is a contemporary issue that evokes a strong response in you?
> (such as homelessness, poverty, abortion, politics)
>
> _____
>
> _____
>
> _____

Step #2: Commit to Prayer
(Nehemiah 1:5-11)

Once Nehemiah sees the need and decides to care, he commits to prayer. His object
of care becomes his object of prayer. What he sees drives him to his knees. A closer look
at the content of his prayer can help you learn how to pray about your life purpose.

First, he remembers his source. Nehemiah begins his prayer, "*O Lord, God of heaven,
the great and awesome God*" (v. 5). Nehemiah does not move an inch to fix the problem
without first acknowledging his source of strength. He knows building a wall around
Jerusalem is out of his league, but not God's. The logistics of successfully accomplishing
a project of this scope and magnitude are mind-boggling. It is nothing short of a miracle
that Nehemiah does not quit before he starts. There is only one truth that moves him forward. He knows he serves a great and awesome God. He knows his only hope of success
is to tap into the creator of heaven and earth as his ultimate source of power.

Have you made the same discovery? Have you determined not to move an inch toward your life purpose without first acknowledging Almighty God as the essential and
ultimate power source of your life? *With God all things are possible*. This great truth runs like
a golden thread from Genesis to Revelation. Successful people discover this promise and
live by it; failures disdain it and are defeated without it. It is the fool who moves forward
without God as the source of power.

In May of 1945, Russian soldiers marched into Berlin. Many of these soldiers had
never seen a large city. Some had never seen electric lights or water faucets. They thought
the gadgets carried their own power, so they pocketed the light bulbs and faucets for
instant light and water for the future. There was only one problem – they had left behind

_ of power.

.us reminds his followers, *"I am the vine; you are the branches. If a man remains in me . I in him, he will bear much fruit; apart from me you can do nothing"* (John 15:5). You must never make the mistake of running ahead into your life purpose, but leaving behind your power source.

God-sized dreams require a God powerful enough to fuel the project. Without a vision of God's unlimited power, the temptation will be to reduce the size of the dream by trimming it down to match your limited human power and ability. Instead of having faith in the God of the impossible, fear of failure moves in with its paralyzing grip.

Imagine what would have happened if Nehemiah had failed to see God as great and awesome? Chances are the building project would have never been started, much less finished. The God-sized dream of a fortified wall around Jerusalem would have become nothing more than a set of rolled-up blueprints in a drawer. I wonder how many God-inspired life missions are stuffed in drawers.

Life missions get exciting when the dream is clearly beyond human ability, when the only hope of the dream being fulfilled is if God shows up. Dare to dream big by dreaming beyond yourself. Believe in a God who *"is able to do immeasurably more than we ask or imagine, according to his power that is at work with us"* (Ephesians 3:20). Who wants to follow a God the size of a human? Follow a God who is huge, massive, gigantic.

This is where Nehemiah can be of enormous help at the front end of finding your life purpose. Don't try to accomplish your life purpose in your own strength or with your own resources. Don't rush off to achieve your mission in life and leave behind your source of power. Remember, God is the ultimate source of everything you will need for the task. Since God is the one inspiring your dream, it only makes sense that he would also be the one to empower it. What God guides, God provides!

How has God helped you fulfill a dream?

_____

_____

_____

_____

_____

Second, he makes himself available. Nehemiah is 800 miles from Jerusalem with no mention of vacation time or sick leave, but in his time of prayer he is asking God to use him. What a great attitude in seeking God's intervention in your life purpose. I wonder how many of us sound more like Moses when God called him. *Here am I; send Aaron!* The secret to finding your life purpose is not so much your capability as it is your availability. Have you sincerely made yourself available to God to fulfill the dream he has inspired within you?

One might think that the great heroes of the Bible were men and women of incredible ability. Looking at their accomplishments recorded in the Scripture might lead you to believe they had superhuman skills. But take a closer look at the likes of Abraham, David, Jeremiah, Isaiah, John the Baptist, Mary, Peter and Paul. Certainly they all had certain abilities. But superhuman? Look again. Look closely and you will find glaring deficiencies and potentially crippling inadequacies.

How did they pull it off? How were they able to accomplish so much for God? If their secret was not found in their incredible skills and abilities, where was it found? Look carefully and you will find the common denominator was in their availability. When God called, they showed up. Perhaps Isaiah spoke for them all when he said, "*Here am I; send me.*"

Are you willing to echo the words of Isaiah as God calls you on a journey to find and fulfill your life mission? God is a magnificent source of power, but he is looking for willing vessels. The Scriptures are clear that God can and does use all kinds of vessels to accomplish his work in the world – young and old, rich and poor, educated and uneducated, male and female. But in order for God to use a vessel, it must be willing. Be a willing vessel like Nehemiah by making yourself available. When God puts the big ask on you, respond with the big yes to his call.

What are some practical ways you can make yourself more available to God?

_____

_____

_____

_____

Third, he asks for success. Are you sometimes too bashful in prayer? Are you afraid to ask God for the impossible, even though Scripture teaches that God does the impossible (cf. Matthew 19:26; Ephesians 3:20)? This is not the case with Nehemiah as he prays,

"Give your servant success today by granting him favor" (v. 11). Be like Nehemiah in boldly asking God for his favor and success. Approach the throne of God with confidence. Let the words of Paul given to Timothy guide you. *"For God did not give us a spirit of timidity, but a spirit of power, of love and of self-discipline"* (II Timothy 1:7). Learn to pray boldly.

How long should you anticipate praying boldly before God starts you on the road to fulfilling your life purpose? We find the answer by taking a closer look at the timeline of events in chapter 2. In verse 11, Nehemiah asks God to give him success today. According to verse one, this is in the month of Kislev. However, according to chapter two God does not open the door of opportunity until the month of Nisan. This is four months later. One of the great ironies of Nehemiah's story is that the construction of the wall only takes 52 days. The preparation of prayer takes four months. Pray boldly, pray with confidence and pray with perseverance.

> God has great plans for your life. He is ready and willing to provide the resources needed to fulfill that plan.

Have you learned the power in praying boldly and expecting God to answer? The story is told of a deeply devoted Christian lady who lived next door to an atheist. She was always praising God for answering her prayers and providing for her needs. One day her atheist neighbor decided to play a trick on her. He had overheard her praying for groceries for the week. While she was taking her afternoon nap, he went to the store and bought a bag of groceries and put it on her front porch. He then rang the doorbell and hid behind the bushes. When she opened the door and saw the groceries, she began to praise God. Her neighbor jumped out from behind the bushes and said, "I tricked you. I bought the groceries. It wasn't your God answering your prayers. It was me!" But the woman continued to praise God. The atheist said, "Why are you still praising God when you know I purchased the groceries?" The woman responded, "Not only did God provide my groceries; he had the Devil pay the bill!"

God has great plans for your life. He is ready and willing to provide the resources needed to fulfill that plan. In Jeremiah 29:11, God declares his desires for us as believers. *"'For I know the plans I have for you,' declares the LORD, 'plans to prosper you and not to harm you, plans to give you hope and a future.'"* Are you genuinely committed to praying for God's direction in regard to your life purpose? Are you convinced that God is for you and will be the ultimate source of your success? Have you sincerely made yourself available to God's plans and purposes? Catching God's vision for your life purpose begins when you commit to prayer.

How is God presently involved in your goals and life purpose?

_____

_____

_____

_____

_____

How are you specifically relying upon God for success with your life purpose?

_____

_____

_____

Step #3: Begin to Prepare
(Nehemiah 2:1-10)

Nehemiah is praying, but he is praying with his eyes open. He is waiting and watching for God to open a door of opportunity. This is not an easy task for a man of action like Nehemiah. He has things to do, people to see and a wall to build. It must have been extremely difficult, bordering on painful, to wait for this opportunity to present itself. This is where patience becomes a required virtue for the journey. You must be willing to wait for God's timing. Allow God the necessary time to work behind the scenes, preparing the hearts of key people. Instead of trying to kick down the door of opportunity, wait for God to prepare the way.

When the door finally swings open, Nehemiah is ready with a three-fold petition. Listen carefully to his specific requests. It sounds like Nehemiah has been carefully preparing his speech while he waited for this God-orchestrated access to the king.

First, he asks permission. Nehemiah cannot make a move without the permission of King Artaxerxes. But when the opportunity arises, Nehemiah is ready with his first request. *"If it pleases the king and if your servant has found favor in his sight, let him send me to the city in Judah where my fathers are buried so that I can rebuild it"* (v. 5).

In fulfilling your life purpose, you may have to get permission from key people in your life. Do you know who they are? Have you carefully and intentionally identified who they are and why they belong on your key-people list? The list may include parents or a spouse, a pastor or a ministry leader. It could include a board of directors or a group of potential donors. The wisdom of Nehemiah is clear: don't run ahead without the permission of key people. Very often God will use key people as a caution light. Their purpose may not be to stop your life mission, but as a proceed-with-caution warning to make sure you are in step with God's timing. In the case of Nehemiah, the king provides a green light for the project.

> Whose permission do you need to fulfill your life purpose?
>
> _____
>
> _____

Second, he asks for provision. Nehemiah does not have access to the construction materials he will need to build the wall, but the King does. *"And may I have a letter to Asaph, keeper of the king's forest, so he will give me timber to make beams for the gates of the citadel by the temple and for the city wall and for the residence I will occupy?"* (v. 8).

When it comes to fulfilling your life purpose, God has a marvelous and mysterious way of providing needed resources along the way. You may be shocked and surprised at the people God will use to help you fulfill your mission. Chances are remote that you will have all the required resources at the beginning of the journey. This is because God loves surprises. He loves to surprise his people along the way with unexpected provisions from unexpected people. Some of your most faith-building experiences in your life mission adventure will be when God surprises you with provisions. So, don't be afraid to ask.

> What provisions do you need or lack in fulfilling your life purpose?
>
> _____
>
> _____
>
> _____
>
> _____
>
> _____

Who are the people who could provide these resources?

_____

_____

_____

_____

Third, he asks for protection. Nehemiah faces a dangerous journey and the certainty of opposition once he arrives (you will learn more about these enemies, Sanballat and Tobiah, later). Nehemiah makes a request of the king. *"If it pleases the king, may I have letters to the governors of Trans-Euphrates, so that they will provide me safe-conduct until I arrive in Judah?"* (v. 7).

In your journey to find and fulfill your life purpose, you can expect opposition along the way. It may seem difficult to understand now, but not everyone will be cheering for your success. The challenge is to understand the reality of opposition and expect its arrival. This allows you to seek God's divine protection from the very beginning. Jesus said, *"In this world you will have tribulation, but be of good cheer. I have overcome the world"* (John 16:33). The Apostle Paul reminds us, *"Everyone who wants to live a godly life in Christ Jesus will be persecuted"* (II Timothy 3:12). Expect opposition. It comes with the territory. But remember, God is in the overcoming business, so you can trust him to provide protection for the journey.

Preparing for your life purpose is much like a contractor preparing a set of blueprints for a building. A contractor would never begin constructing a building without first having a thorough set of blueprints. There will come a day when the saws and hammers come out of the tool chests and the actual construction begins. But not until adequate preparations are complete.

The same is true for your life mission. The preparation phase is crucial for the successful construction of a sound life purpose. But here is where some people make a critical mistake. They don't take the necessary time to prepare. Most people do not plan to fail; they just fail to plan. Not so with Nehemiah. While he prays, he begins to prepare.

Have you started to prepare for your life purpose? It helps to start writing down your thoughts and ideas. Go back over Nehemiah's preparations and see where he can instruct and inspire you. Spending time with a close friend or finding a qualified life coach can be a valuable investment in this process. Sometimes a new set of eyes and ears can provide clarity to your dream; catching God's vision for your life purpose starts when you begin to prepare.

13

Even if you currently are unclear about your specific life purpose, what are you doing right now to become the person God can trust to fulfill his purposes?

_____

_____

_____

_____

_____

_____

_____

_____

Like Nehemiah, are you becoming a person who is dependable, honest, honorable, and respectful of authority? Have the people surrounding you placed their absolute trust in your character?

_____

_____

_____

_____

_____

Living My Dash: Catching God's Vision

I began to live out my life purpose in 1998. That was the year I resigned as the co-pastor of a church in Roswell, New Mexico, a church I helped plant and in which I served for 19 years. It was without a doubt the most difficult time in my life. But through the miracle of 20/20 hindsight, I now see it was the most significant turning point in finding and fulfilling my life purpose. God has a wonderful way of bringing gold out of the refiner's fire.

A small group of people approached me about planting a new church in Roswell. Starting a new church was not something on my before-I-die bucket list. But I agreed to at least pray about the possibility. It was during this time that God spoke to me in an unusual and unexpected way — through a book. I had heard about a book called *The Purpose-Driven Church*, written by some pastor in California named Rick Warren. I knew nothing about Rick Warren, but I decided this might be a good book to read if I was giving serious consideration to planting a new church.[2]

So, I called my friend who owned the local Christian book store in town to order a copy of the book. Before I could mention the title, my friend said, "I was about to call you. Something very unusual just happened here at the bookstore. A man who used to be a pastor in Roswell was driving through town, dropped into the bookstore, and asked about you. I told him you were considering planting a new church. He immediately walked over to one of my bookshelves, picked up a book and bought it for you. But he gave me instructions that I was not to reveal his identity to you. He wanted the gift to be anonymous." I told the owner I would drop by later to get the mystery book, but I needed him to order a copy of *The Purpose-Driven Church*. There was silence on the other end of the phone. Finally, he said, "Rick, this is the book the pastor bought for you!" At that moment, I realized God might be up to something.

To make a long story short, I read the book and knew God was calling me to plant a purpose-driven church in Roswell. So much of what Rick Warren shared in his book resonated with my spirit. This was the kind of church I wanted to plant and lead. That was 1998. The new purpose-driven church was planted and is still thriving today. In fact, God has further clarified and expanded the vision of our church to reach 10 percent of our community for Christ. This is our life purpose as a church family. We are well into the journey and have already reached over one-third of our goal. I am having the time of my life living out my life purpose with a group of godly people who share the vision with me. It all started when I caught God's vision for my life purpose.

I am convinced God has a mission for your life, too. God has a task he wants you to complete between now and your funeral. For Nehemiah, the mission was building a wall around Jerusalem. For me, it is building a church to reach 10 percent of my community for Christ. What is your life purpose? Whatever it is, the first step in discovering your mission is to catch God's vision. Decide to care, commit to prayer and begin to prepare. It worked for Nehemiah, it is working for me, and it will work for you. Catch God's vision and you will be on your way to living your dash.

I have included several Action Steps below. Take some time to read and think through each step and how it applies to you. Each step is designed to prayerfully guide you to catch God's vision for your life purpose.

Chapter 1: Catch God's Vision

Step #1: Decide to Care (Nehemiah 1:1-4)

I acknowledge that God created me uniquely, with inherent passions and dreams. What matters most to me was divinely placed in my heart by God and is a good indication of God's life purpose for me.

Step #2: Commit to Prayer (Nehemiah 1:5-11)

Instead of rushing ahead of God, I commit to pray intently for clarity concerning anything God reveals to me as a potential life purpose. As God brings clarity of vision, I can boldly ask for his power and provision to fulfill my life purpose. As I wait for clarity and direction, I also commit to make myself fully available to God for whatever life purpose he reveals.

Step #3: Begin to Prepare (Nehemiah 2:1-10)

I resolve to be fully prepared for the life purpose to which God calls me. I understand that part of this preparation may involve my personal and professional development long before I have a clear understanding of God's plan for my life.

Father God,

I praise you as the God of all creation and the Creator of all life purposes. I thank you for creating me uniquely with a heart and mind that is moved by various things. Help me discern the uniqueness of my individual design and purpose. Reveal to me your divine power to fulfill the specific call you have placed on my life. Empower me to make myself fully available to you. Help prepare me both personally and professionally for the specific life purpose to which you are calling me.

In Jesus name I pray, Amen.

CHAPTER TWO

CONFIRM YOUR LIFE PURPOSE

The most powerful weapon on earth is the human soul on fire.
Field Marshall Ferdinand Foch

The key to successful leadership today is influence, not authority.
Ken Blanchard

Finding your life purpose requires that you first catch God's vision for what He wants to accomplish through you. At this point in the journey, you will not know all the details of the picture; just the broad strokes of God's plan. Don't worry about the unknowns. There will be plenty of time for God to add the needed color and texture to the painting of his masterpiece we are calling your life purpose. For now be patient, focus your attention on the big picture and don't sweat the details.

Life purposes are as numerous and diverse as people. We are talking about a God who never replicates a snow flake or a fingerprint. God loves diversity and creativity. He has a wonderful habit of uniquely shaping each person for a different life purpose. Imagine for a moment the possible unique shape of your life mission. It may involve children or teenagers, senior citizens or singles, the disabled or the divorced. It could extend to serving the homeless or the grieving, the addict or the dying. The list of possibilities is as long as the unmet needs around you or even around the world. Isn't this at the heart of Paul's words, *"For we are God's workmanship, created in Christ Jesus to do good works, which God prepared in advance for us to do"*(Ephesians 2:10). What an awesome privilege to realize that the creator of the universe has chosen to do his work through us and has uniquely fashioned us to accomplish this good work.

But what happens when you begin to sense the specific life purpose God has written beside your name? A day will come when what was once a blurry vision comes into focus. Then it is time for the mission to move forward and progress to the next natural level. A God-vision once caught cannot remain stagnant. It is a living sort of thing that should not be caged or it will die. It requires movement, growth and development. What is the next step in this journey of getting better connected to your specific mission?

Your life purpose seeks to meet the needs of what type of person?

_____

_____

_____

_____

The second major step in the life purpose journey involves confirmation. This step is designed to move you beyond how you feel to what others think. What do the significant people in your life think about your vision? Does it resonate in their hearts? Do they respond with words of confirmation or with looks of confusion? Do they jump on board to partner with you in fulfilling your dream or do they jump ship? It is crucial at this stage of the process that you are willing to do the difficult, and often uncomfortable, work of confirmation. There is no doubt about it; confirmation is demanding. Sometimes the significant people in your life will tell you what you need to hear instead of what you want to hear. Their honest reaction to your dream is important for you to consider.

When you have shared elements of your life purpose with family and close friends, what type of reaction did you receive?

_____

_____

_____

_____

In the beginning pages of Nehemiah's story, you see him catching a vision of God's plan and purpose for his life. The vision is clear, concise and compelling. He is to build a wall around Jerusalem. You might expect to see a "get-it-done" kind of guy like Nehemiah to charge off to Jerusalem, toolbox in hand, to start rebuilding the wall. But this does not happen. At this early stage in his journey, Nehemiah demonstrates great wisdom.

Before he ever turns a spade of dirt or lifts a single rock, Nehemiah confirms his life purpose. This critical stage of his adventure is told in chapters two and three of his journal. Here Nehemiah teaches three essential steps that can help you learn the how and why of confirming your life purpose.

Step #1: Evaluation (Nehemiah 2:11-16)

You have probably heard of the midnight ride of Paul Revere. Well, here you read the story of the midnight ride of Nehemiah. His first act after arriving in Jerusalem is to inspect the condition of the wall he has been commissioned to rebuild. He conducts his inspection at night, accompanied by only a few men. Nehemiah makes a statement which sounds strange at first. *"I had not told anyone what my God had put in my heart to do for Jerusalem"* (2:12). In other words, he did not immediately announce his life purpose publically. Going public would come later, but first things first. Initially, he had to conduct an honest evaluation of the situation. His goal is to gain a realistic picture of the task before him.

What do Proverbs 17:27 and 29:20 teach us about waiting to declare publically our life purpose?

_____

_____

_____

_____

What are some possible side-effects of going public too early with your life purpose?

_____

_____

_____

_____

_____

_____

Here Nehemiah teaches the first confirmation principle. *Honestly evaluate the challenge before you and the resources available to you.* It pays to invest the time to inspect and to do the research before you invest the money and energy to fulfill your mission. The key word is before. Many life missions have been unnecessarily shipwrecked because an honest, realistic evaluation was bypassed. You probably know of situations where well-meaning people moved too fast or too soon into a project, a business or a ministry.

Honest evaluation needs to take place before you invest too much time, talent and treasure. When you fail to evaluate at the front end, you greatly increase the risk of failure at the back end. Ask yourself the hard questions. How will this affect my family? What kind of resources will I need? How long will it take to get my dream off the ground? Am I willing to pay the price and do whatever it takes to get the job done? Are there any obstacles I have not considered? Am I being honest with myself as I answer these questions?

Honest evaluation in no way contradicts or undermines your faith in God. A good dose of realism can actually confirm your faith and help firmly plant your faith in God in the soil of reality. The goal is to avoid being so heavenly minded that you are of no earthly good. It is good and godly to count the cost.

Jesus once challenged a large crowd of would-be followers to first count the cost before signing on the dotted line of discipleship. He confronts them with a penetrating question. *"Suppose one of you wants to build a tower. Will he not first sit down and estimate the cost to see if he has enough money to complete it?"* (Luke 14:28).

The time for going public with your vision will come later. First, make sure an honest and realistic evaluation is done regarding the scope and cost of the project. Pull off the rose-colored glasses before you begin this process. You must be brutally honest with yourself. Do you know the costs and are you willing to pay the price? Self-deception at this point in the journey is deadly and is sure to sink your ship.

What are some of the costs associated with fulfilling your life purpose?

_____

_____

_____

Step #2: Presentation (Nehemiah 2:17-20)

Once Nehemiah's inspection tour is complete, he is ready to share his vision with others. Now it is time to go public. He clearly understands that the task of rebuilding the wall without the help of others is impossible. He needs to have confirmation and buy-in from the key individuals who will be directly involved in the building project. If they are not onboard with the vision, Nehemiah's ship will never be able to leave the dock, much less successfully sail to its destination.

Who are the key individuals from whom you need confirmation and buy-in?

_____

_____

_____

_____

Nehemiah's presentation must do more than just motivate his potential team. It must also educate them. Nehemiah must lay out the vision with enough detail that others can begin to catch the overall vision. Here he must begin to answer and clarify the what, how and why questions of the potential members of his building team. Specifically, Nehemiah must address three crucial concerns. When you begin to share your vision with others, your presentation needs to answer these same three questions.

Question #1: What is the specific vision to be accomplished?

Nehemiah clarifies that his vision is to rebuild the wall around the city of Jerusalem. *"You see the trouble we are in: Jerusalem lies in ruins, and its gates have been burned with fire. Come, let us rebuild the wall of Jerusalem and we will no longer be in disgrace"* (v. 17). You must be sure to clarify your vision and carefully explain what you hope to accomplish with your life purpose. No one is motivated to get on the train if they don't know where the train is going. Be clear, be specific and be focused in clarifying your vision. Nehemiah is able to share his vision in a couple of sentences. Can you do the same with your vision?

> *You must be sure to clarify your vision and carefully explain what you hope to accomplish with your life purpose. No one is motivated to get on the train if they don't know where the train is going.*

Often more clarity will come with time, but currently what do you see as your life purpose?

_____

_____

_____

_____

_____

Question #2: How will the vision be accomplished?

Nehemiah makes it clear that he needs their help rebuilding the wall. He cannot do the job alone. It will require a team working together to accomplish the task. He then wisely describes what God has already done in regard to the king providing the necessary supplies. *"I also told them about the gracious hand of my God upon me and what the king had said to me"* (v. 18).

You must never be afraid to ask for help. A life purpose involving only you is not big enough. Dream big. Don't put limitations on what God wants to accomplish through you with the involvement of others. But how can you inspire others to catch the vision and get involved? Do what Nehemiah does. Tell your story. Tell others what God has already done for you. Nothing will inspire and motivate others more than hearing the mighty acts of God in your life. This is why King David and the other psalmists repeatedly challenge God's people throughout the Psalms to tell of the mighty acts of God and proclaim his powerful deeds. *"Give thanks to the Lord, call on his name; make known among the nations what he has done. Sing to him, sing praises to him; tell of all his wonderful acts"* (Psalm 105:1-2). People may argue with a sermon, but they can't argue with your story. Be ready to tell others how the gracious hand of God has already been preparing and guiding you toward your life purpose.

How has God's provision for you in the past confirmed your life purpose?

_____

_____

Question #3: Why should you accomplish the vision?

People want to know why your mission is important, so you better be able to tell them. Nehemiah's appeal is two-fold: he appeals to their national pride and to their faith in God. *It is time to end our public disgrace; God has already confirmed his presence with us. We must rebuild this wall!* The Jews living in a wall-less Jerusalem are being publically humiliated by their enemies. Their living condition is a total disgrace. God has clearly confirmed his presence in Nehemiah's vision to rebuild the wall, so there is no excuse for leaving their city unprotected.

People want and need to know why your vision matters. They want to know if their investment and involvement will make an eternal difference. People need to be convinced that your dream is God-inspired and God-empowered. There are thousands of causes and projects begging people for their investment and involvement. Why should they say yes to your request? Before you put the big ask on people for help, you must first answer the big *why* question.

Why should other people want to invest their time, talent, and treasure into helping fulfill your vision?

_____

_____

_____

_____

_____

Here you learn the second confirmation principle. *Share your vision with significant others.* What happens if the people who know you best react negatively to your vision? What if there is no buy-in and no one gets on board? What if the only response you receive after sharing your vision is a deer-in-the-headlights look? Then the next step is re-evaluation! You would do well to back up the train and make sure you heard God accurately. This does not mean total failure and the end of the dream, but it does suggest the need for a season of honest re-evaluation to make sure the train is on the right track.

Does this mean you should expect 100 percent affirmation to your vision? Absolutely not. Even Nehemiah received mixed reviews with the initial sharing of his vision. Just like Nehemiah, you can expect the same two responses when you share your vision with others: excitement and opposition. Some people will be with you and ready to support your vision. *"They replied, 'Let us start rebuilding.' So they began this good work"* (v. 18). It is

> *Here is a lesson you must hear loud and clear: don't expect unanimous affirmation and applause when you share your dream.*

exciting and motivating to receive this response. However, others will say, "Are you crazy? There is no way you can accomplish that task!" Listen to Nehemiah's critics. *"But when Sanballat the Horonite, Tobiah the Ammonite official and Geshem the Arab heard about it, they mocked and ridiculed us. 'What is this you are doing?' they asked. 'Are you rebelling against the king?'"* (v. 19).

Here is a lesson you must hear loud and clear: don't expect unanimous affirmation and applause when you share your dream. There will always be critics in the crowd ready to disparage and deflate your dream. Speaking of critics, don't be surprised if your greatest opposition comes from close friends and members of your own family. Jesus was correct when he said, *"A prophet is without honor in his own country."*

This is where wise discernment must be used on your part. Ask yourself, who are the negative voices? Why are they opposed to my vision? Are their concerns legitimate? If their concerns hold merit, address them. If adjustments need to be made in your initial plans, swallow your pride and make the changes. Now is the best time for these kinds of adjustments. But if the concerns are not legitimate, then move forward. Don't let negative critics derail your life purpose. Nehemiah does not let his critics slow him down, and neither should you. Listen carefully to Nehemiah's response to his critics. *"The God of heaven will give us success. We his servants will start rebuilding, but as for you, you have no share in Jerusalem or any claim or historic right to it"* (v. 20).

What opposition have you already experienced or expect to experience in regard to your life purpose?

_____

_____

_____

_____

When I think of meeting opposition and ridicule from negative critics, I am reminded of the words written by Edgar A. Guest.

Somebody said that it couldn't be done,
But he with a chuckle replied
That maybe it couldn't, but he would be one
Who wouldn't say so 'till he tried.

So he buckled right in with the trace of a grin
If he worried, he certainly hid it.
He started to sing as he tackled the thing
That couldn't be done, and he did it.
Somebody scoffed, "Oh, you'll never do that;
At least no one ever has done it."
But he took off his coat and took off his hat
And the first thing you know he'd begun it.

With the lift of his chin and a bit of a grin,
Without any doubting or quiddit,
He started to sing as he tackled the thing
That couldn't be done and he did it.

There are thousands to tell you it cannot be done,
There are thousands who prophesy failure.
There are thousands to point out to you, one by one,
The dangers that wait to assail you.

But just buckle right in with a bit of a grin,
Then take off your coat and go to it.
Just start in to sing as you tackle the thing
That cannot be done and you'll do it.[3]

Step #3: Delegation (Nehemiah 3)

The time finally arrives for Nehemiah to actually begin the work of rebuilding the wall. But Nehemiah's earlier inspection tour clearly reveals the enormity of the task. He cannot do the job alone, so he begins to recruit others and delegate responsibilities. Chapter three records the various responsibilities delegated by Nehemiah to his team of volunteers. Notice the recurring phrase, *"next to him...next to him...next to him,"* throughout the chapter. This is definitely a team project with people working together to get the job done.

It is interesting to see some of the specific assignments given by Nehemiah in chapter three. The priests and Levites roll up their sleeves and get their hands dirty (v. 1). How refreshing to see the religious leaders leading by example. People are not impressed with "do as I say, not as I do" leaders. These priests and Levites are not afraid to put on a hard hat and do manual labor. Did you also notice that no one is left out who wants to serve? Even the goldsmiths and perfumers are doing their part (v. 8). You may be pleasantly surprised in fulfilling your life purpose to see unexpected participants show up and offer their support.

It is impressive that this building project is not reserved for the select few. A place is made for men, women and even the children to be involved in the project (v. 12). Of course, not everyone is willing to serve. There are some lazy nobles who consider themselves above common labor. *"The next section was repaired by the men of Tekoa, but their nobles would not put their shoulders to the work under their supervisors"* (v. 5). You can expect to find the same problem today. Lazy is still alive and well on planet earth!

This next one may surprise you, but I hope it inspires you. One of the rulers, named Malkijah, has a special assignment. His task is to rebuild the Dung Gate. *"The Dung Gate was repaired by Malkijah son of Recab, ruler of the district of Beth Hakkerem. He rebuilt it and put its doors and bolts and bars in place"* (v. 14). Yes, you read that right. This humble ruler volunteers to repair the gate to the toilet. Somebody has to do the dirty work that no one else wants to do, so Malkijah signs up for the job. Personally, if I had been Nehemiah, I would have assigned this job to the perfumers!

You have just observed one of the great leadership principles in the Bible: *the importance of delegation.* The successful leaders in the Bible learn and practice the art of delegating. We see examples of delegation in both Old and New Testaments. For example, Moses learns the lesson of delegation from his father-in-law, Jethro. The story is told in Exodus 18. At this point in the Biblical narrative, Moses is leading the Israelites through the wilderness, but the job is just about to get the best of him. The demands of the people are coming at him non-stop and the great man of God is nearing burnout. Jethro sees what is happening to his son-in-law and intervenes with wisdom that can be summarized in one word: delegate.

Jethro convinces the weary and worn-out Moses to select other leaders to whom he can delegate some of the leadership responsibilities. Moses takes the advice and it works. The needs of the people are met and Moses regains his sanity.

We see this same principle of delegation at work in the New Testament. One such example is seen in the early days of the church when the church in Jerusalem is experiencing a time of explosive growth. In Acts 4 the church has already grown to about 5,000 members and this is just counting the men. Add in the women and children and you definitely have the makings of a mega-church, which also creates mega-problems.

One such mega-problem surfaces in Acts 6. Apparently a conflict arises between the Grecian Jewish Christians and the Hebraic Jewish Christians in the Jerusalem church. The conflict is over the issue of food distribution to the widows from the two groups. This conflict has the potential to split the Jerusalem Church right down party lines. Faced with this problem, the Apostles move quickly and wisely use delegation to solve the problem. Seven deacons are selected and given the authority to handle the widow problem. This allows the Apostles to refocus their attention on their primary responsibilities of prayer and teaching.

Tragically, we still see churches today failing to take advantage of the Biblical principle of delegation. Someone has compared the church to a football game where 50,000 people in the stands that are in desperate need of exercise watch 11 men on the field who are in desperate need of rest. This is all too often repeated in churches today where leaders are too controlling and try to micro-manage everything.

When I hear stories of leaders who refuse to delegate because they want to be in charge, it reminds me of what was said of President Franklin D. Roosevelt. He was known as a person who loved to be in charge and enjoyed being the center of attention. One of his own children jokingly said of him, "My father would love to be the bride at every wedding and the corpse at every funeral."

Leaders must be willing to delegate, joyfully giving the ministry to the members and members must be willing to give the leadership responsibilities to the leaders. When this does not happen, the results in the local church are tragic. We see overworked leaders burnout and inactive members rust out. There has to be a better way and that way is delegation. What is true of the church is also true with your life purpose. Learn the value of involving others.

Here you learn the third confirmation principle. *Don't try to fulfill your life mission alone; build a team.* You will do life better together. This is never more evident than when you are finding and fulfilling your life mission. Do not miss the joy, fulfillment and fun that await you when you work together as a team to accomplish a great work for God. There is great joy in the journey when you travel together as a team. Find other qualified leaders, train them and then delegate responsibilities to them.

It would be easy for Nehemiah during his midnight ride to look at the enormity of the task and quit before he ever gets started. But he wisely chooses another path. After a thorough and honest evaluation of the situation, he presents his vision to others with passion and clarity. Once they are onboard with the vision, he begins to delegate the essential responsibilities to key individuals.

We must not miss the essential ingredient in Nehemiah's character: perseverance. In the face of enormous odds against him, he moves forward with perseverance and determination. Nehemiah is going to build that wall, and at this point, the gates of hell will not prevail against him.

What could possibly derail you from staying on track with your life purpose?

_____

_____

_____

_____

Nehemiah's perseverance reminds me of another great man of God who refused to throw in the towel. John Wesley had a vision of sharing the Gospel of Jesus Christ with the lost, but getting this vision off the ground was not easy at the beginning. The following entries are taken from his diary:

- Sunday morning, May 5, preached in St. Ann's and was asked not to come back anymore.
- Sunday evening, May 5, preached at St. John's; deacons said, "Get out and stay out!"
- Sunday morning, May 12, preached at St. Jude's; can't go back there either.
- Sunday evening, May 12, preached at St. George's; kicked out again.
- Sunday morning, May 19, preached at St. somebody else's; deacons called a special meeting and said I couldn't return.
- Sunday evening, May 19, preached on the street; kicked off the street.
- Sunday morning, May 26, preached in meadow; chased out of the meadow as a bull was turned loose during the services.
- Sunday morning, June 2, preached out at the edge of town; kicked off the highway.
- Sunday evening, June 2, afternoon service; preached in a pasture; 10,000 people came to hear me.[4]

John Wesley learned what Nehemiah learned and what you must learn. It takes persistence to find and fulfill your life purpose. It pays to persevere. Success for you may be just one diary entry away.

Just like Nehemiah built a dream team to help him accomplish his life purpose, who are some people (or types of people) you need on your dream team?

_____

_____

_____

_____

Living My Dash: Confirming God's Vision

Planting a new church was not what I had planned on doing at the age of 44. I can assure you it was not on my five-year planner. I had helped plant a church 19 years earlier, so I knew the difficulty of getting a church off the ground. In many ways, church planting is best played as a young man's game. Plus, I had a wife, two teenagers and a mortgage. I honestly did not know if I was cut out for another church plant.

I also realized this would be a totally different experience. My first church plant began with 30 people and grew to 1,300 members over a 19 year period. Growth had been slow and steady, allowing for calm and consistent assimilation of new members. This new church had the potential of starting with several hundred members from day one. I would have to rapidly build ministries from scratch to support an instant church. This would require large numbers of trained and equipped volunteer leaders since I was the only pastor. I would definitely be travelling into unchartered territory if I accepted the job. Before I signed on the dotted line to plant this church, I needed confirmation.

Our first meeting was in a home. From my previous experience in planting a church, I knew a new congregation needed around 40 to 50 people to be viable in our community. So, I prayed, "God, if 40 people show up for the first service, I will take that as a good sign of confirmation." Was I ever surprised when 90 people crammed into the house on the first Sunday. But the question was, "Would they all come back the second week?" I prayed, "God, if all 90 people come back next Sunday, I will take that as a good sign of confirmation." We rented a banquet room at a local hotel for the second Sunday. Was I ever surprised when over 200 people came the second Sunday and the third Sunday. Every time I prayed for confirmation, God doubled my expectations. I felt a bit like Gideon every Sunday after service as I checked the moisture content of my fleece.

I shared my vision with the people every Sunday for two months. It was a vision of planting a church for unchurched people with the goal of helping them discover God's plan and purpose for their lives. In some ways, I felt like Nehemiah. I saw the need in my community for this kind of church, but I knew I could never pull this off alone. I needed to know if there was buy-in. I felt a strong leading from God, but I still needed confirmation from the people.

During the third month, I decided it was time to invite people to sign the official charter if they were on board with the vision. Guided once again by the example of Nehemiah, I spelled out as clearly and honestly as I could the realistic challenges of planting a new church. I wanted potential members to be well aware of what they were getting themselves into before they made their final commitment. Starting a church can be exciting at the beginning, during the honeymoon period. But I knew from experience what was coming after the new-and-exciting had worn off. I knew that getting this church off the ground would not be an easy task.

I refused to sugar-coat the vision. People needed to understand the hassle of meeting in rented facilities without adequate classrooms for their children and teenagers. They needed to understand that being a portable church involved setting up and tearing down week after week, possibly for years. It would require opening their homes for adult classes and small groups. It would demand large numbers of volunteers to lead the various ministries. Above all, it would mean serving and sacrificing at a level some of them had never experienced.

At the end of the third month, we gathered for a special Sunday service. I invited people to come forward and sign the official church covenant. But I only invited people to come forward if, after serious prayer, they were confident that God was leading them to make this commitment. I then prayed and waited. I will never forget standing in front of the auditorium next to the table displaying the covenant. I honestly had no idea what would happen next. All I knew is that later that day, I would either be leading a new church or updating my resume.

Then it happened. One by one, people started coming forward. I couldn't believe my eyes as a line began to form in front of the table and soon circled around the back of the room. Person after person, family after family took pen in hand and signed their names to the document. At the end of the service, 412 people had signed the document. The framed charter now hangs in the hallway of our worship center, a continual reminder of the faithfulness of God and a personal reminder to me of the value of confirmation.

Getting your life purpose off the ground can be a huge challenge. It can be like the takeoff of a 747 jetliner. It takes a lot of different people to get a jetliner in the air. Trained crews have to service the engines. Flight attendants have to complete their assigned tasks in the cabin. The pilots must carefully go over their checklists in the cockpit. Even the passengers must have their seat belts buckled and their tray tables in the upright and locked position. Everyone understands the challenge before them. Everyone realizes it is a team effort to get the plane airborne.

Your life purpose is the same. It is not a solo adventure. It is a team sport and a big part of getting your mission airborne involves confirmation. There may be moments when you feel like plans are moving at a snail's pace. You may be tempted to rush in, grab a hammer and start rebuilding the wall. When this temptation hits, remember Nehemiah's example. Wait...slow down...persevere. The time and energy invested at this stage is essential. Once your life purpose is off the ground, you will be glad you did the evaluation, presentation and delegation.

Now that you have caught God's vision and confirmed it, you are on your way to the third major step in living your dash. But before you move to the next chapter, take time to read and pray through the following Action Steps. They are designed to help guide you through the confirmation process.

Chapter 2 – Confirm Your life Purpose

Living Your Dash

Step #1: Evaluation (Nehemiah 2:11-16)
Before going public with my life purpose, I will evaluate the scope of the task, the resources available to me, and the cost of commitment required to accomplish God's purpose for my life.

Step #2: Presentation (Nehemiah 2:17-20)
I will do the required work of preparation, so that when the time comes to present my life purpose it is clear, concise, and contagious.

Step #3: Delegation (Nehemiah 3)
Understanding that I cannot accomplish God's purpose for my life alone, I will build a dream team of individuals to partner with me in accomplishing my life purpose.

Father God,

I praise you for being omniscient (all knowing) and omnipotent (all powerful). Forgive me for the times I rush ahead of you in zealous devotion. Help me to be patient and thorough as I clearly evaluate the cost of following your plans for my life. As I present your vision to others, help it to become clearer and more concise. Bring into my life the various members of my dream team that will help support me in fulfilling my life purpose.

In Jesus name I pray, Amen.

CHAPTER THREE

OVERCOME
EXTERNAL OPPOSITION

Leadership is not a noun; it is a verb. It is not an identity; it is an action.
Rabbi Daniel Lapin

Leadership is the capacity to translate vision into reality.
Warren B. Bennis

S hipping codfish is big business in the northeastern United States. However, the codfish industry faced a challenge in the early days of shipping. There was a great demand inland, but getting the codfish delivered fresh was a difficult challenge. The shippers tried freezing it, but the fish lost much of its flavor. They tried shipping the codfish alive in large tanks of sea water, but this proved to be too expensive and the fish lost much of its flavor and texture. Finally, some creative soul solved the problem. The codfish were placed in large tanks of water along with their natural enemy, the catfish. From the time the codfish left the coast until they arrived inland, those ornery catfish chased the codfish around the tank. The result: when the codfish finally arrived at the market, they were as fresh as when they were first caught, with no loss of flavor. In fact, the texture of the meat had actually improved.

Who are the ornery catfish in your life? Who are the people who think it is their mission in life to oppose you and try to prevent you from fulfilling your life purpose? Are the faces of specific people coming to your mind right now, people who act as if their spiritual gift is to be a pain in your neck? You know who they are. You have probably fantasized about pictures of their faces mounted on a dart board. In your journey to find and fulfill your life purpose, not everyone is going to support you. Not everyone will stand on the sidelines, waving pompoms and cheering for you to succeed. You can expect your share of people to oppose your dreams and criticize your efforts.

An opposition-free life purpose is an oxymoron, especially for the person who is on a quest to accomplish something great for God. The greater the vision, the greater the opposition you can expect. So don't be surprised when the critics show up. Peter affirms this truth when he encourages his first-century Christian readers who are facing opposition for their commitment to Christ. *"Dear friends, do not be surprised at the painful trial you are suffering, as though something strange were happening to you"* (I Peter 4:12). Don't be shocked and surprised when critics appear and begin to take shots at you. Opposition comes with the life purpose territory. It is essential to learn this unpleasant truth toward the front-end of your life mission because external opposition is powerful. It has the ability to deflate a dream. If you are not careful, you can let the negative, critical voices take the wind out of your sails.

Remember the story of Elijah in I Kings 18-19? Elijah is coming off the mountain-top experience of confronting the prophets of Baal on Mount Carmel. With God's miraculous intervention, Elijah is able to defeat and destroy these false prophets. We might think a victory like that would fuel the prophet's spiritual tank for years, but the victorious experience is short-lived. Elijah gets word that the wicked Queen Jezebel is out to get him. She is ticked off because Elijah has killed her prophets of Baal. Her exact words delivered by messenger to Elijah are terrifying. *"May the gods deal with me, be it ever so severely, if by this time tomorrow I do not make your life like that of one of them [the prophets of Baal]"* (I Kings 19:2). How will the great prophet of God respond to this threat?

> Opposition comes with the life purpose territory. It is essential to learn this unpleasant truth toward the front-end of your life mission because external opposition is powerful.

His courage wilts like a flower on a hot summer day. Elijah sits down under a broom tree and prays to die. *"'I have had enough, Lord,' he said. 'Take my life; I am no better than my ancestors'"* (I Kings 19:4). This is one discouraged prophet. Why is he ready to call it quits? He has come face to face with the voice of external opposition. The same can happen to you when critics arise and oppose you. They can create such discouragement that you want to throw in the towel and give up. The ultimate danger is that your mission gets stuffed in a folder and filed away. But your story does not have to end this way. You can overcome the voice of your critics. What can you do to overcome external opposition to your life purpose?

Nehemiah has his share of critics. You met some of his ornery catfish back in chapter two, namely Sanballat the Horonite, Tobiah the Ammonite and Geshem the Arab. These same critics are back in chapter four with a full-out attack with one goal in mind:

to prevent Nehemiah from fulfilling his life purpose. They are committed to bringing the construction project to a halt so that Jerusalem will remain a city without a wall and Nehemiah will remain a leader without an accomplished life purpose. But Nehemiah is ready for their attack. In fact, it appears that he has been expecting their attack. Watch as he implements his successful defensive strategy against his opponents. The plan is carefully designed and masterfully deployed. At the end of the day, Nehemiah's strategy successfully motivates his team and demoralizes his enemies. From his example, you can learn how to successfully develop and implement a plan so that you can overcome external opposition.

Who have been some of the ornery catfish in your life?

_____

_____

_____

_____

Protect Your Vision (Nehemiah 4:1-5)

If you have ever been ridiculed, you know how discouraging it can be. Nothing has the power to pop your balloon of enthusiasm like ridicule. Listen to the mocking ridicule leveled at Nehemiah and his team by his detractors. *"When Sanballat heard that we were rebuilding the wall, he became angry and was greatly incensed. He ridiculed the Jews, and in the presence of his associates and the army of Samaria, he said, 'What are those feeble Jews doing? Will they restore their wall? Will they offer sacrifices? Will they finish in a day? Can they bring the stones back to life from those heaps of rubble – burned as they are?' Tobiah the Ammonite, who was at his side, said, 'What they are building – if even a fox climbed up on it, he would break down their wall of stones!'"* (4:1-3).

Imagine how Nehemiah and his fellow Jews must have felt when they found themselves on the wrong end of this heckling. Take a closer look at their sarcastic remarks and you will see that Nehemiah's critics attack from three specific directions. First, they attack their past achievements. They ridicule, *"If a fox jumps on what you have already built, it will fall down!"* Critics love to point to any weaknesses or failures in your past. Their goal is to focus your attention on the glass being half-empty, or in Nehemiah's case, the wall being half-built. We learn in verse six that the wall at this point has reached the halfway mark, but the critics want to present this fact as a negative, not a positive. Instead of focusing on how much has already been accomplished, the faultfinders concentrate on how much more there is to do. Your critics will do the same. They want you to believe that past flaws and weaknesses are a guarantee of future disasters.

Second, they attack their present weaknesses. They mock, *"You feeble Jews... you don't have what it takes!"* Critics are always happy to point out any weakness in your skill level or that of your team. Granted, this is an easy target for the critics. Nehemiah is a cupbearer and not an architect or contractor. We have already learned in chapter three that Nehemiah is not working with professional wall builders, but with a mixture of priests, farmers, musicians and a few perfumers. Talk about a ready-made target for ridicule. The goal of mockers is always the same: to get a leader and his team focused on what they can't do and on the resources they don't have. If the critics succeed, the team is headed for discouragement and defeat.

Third, they attack their future dreams. They belittle Nehemiah by saying, *"Will you restore the wall? Who are you trying to kid? Your dreams are too big!"* Critics love to deflate your hopes and dreams. They enjoy taking the wind out of your sails so that progress comes to a standstill. Their goal is to make your life mission look impossible and out of reach so that you will quit.

How does Nehemiah respond to his critics? Watch and learn from this master leader. If you like to mark in your Bible, get out your yellow highlighter. This could be a life-changing lesson in your quest to find and fulfill your life purpose. Nehemiah does not turn inward and become discouraged. He does not turn outward, wasting his time attacking his critics. Instead, he turns upward and says, "God, you take care of my critics. I have a wall to build!" Listen carefully to the exact words of his prayer: *"Hear us, O our God, for we are despised. Turn their insults back on their own heads. Give them over to plunder in a land of captivity. Do not cover up their guilt or blot out their sins from your sight, for they have thrown insults in the face of the builders* (vv. 4-5)."

Nehemiah teaches us in two verses the best way to handle critics. Turn upward. He could have easily devised his own negative plan of gossip and ridicule aimed at his critics. He could have rallied his team to mount some sort of attack. Instead, Nehemiah turns to God in prayer and calls on him to take care of his enemies. Learning to replace personal vengeance with prayer is a tough lesson, but a valuable one.

At this point in your journey, it is imperative that you look in the mirror and be brutally honest. Which direction do you turn when you are criticized: inward, outward or upward? This is a question you must be able and willing to answer in the life purpose journey. External opposition will come, so you better decide now how you will respond when it arrives. The options are limited to the three mentioned above: outward, inward or upward.

I have always appreciated the story told about D.L. Moody, the great American evangelist. Moody had his share of critics throughout most of his ministry. At one point in his ministry when criticism was harsh, someone asked him, "Mr. Moody, how have you decided to respond to your critics?" Moody said, "I have decided to stay sweet!" How's

> Moody said, "I have decided to stay sweet!" The best way to stay sweet when being attacked is to turn upward.

that for an upward response? Instead of turning outward and attacking back or turning inward and getting depressed, Moody opted for an upward response. The best way to stay sweet when being attacked is to turn upward.

How will you respond when someone criticizes your life mission? It helps to decide how you will react before the criticism hits. I would highly recommend following Paul's advice given in Romans 12:17-18. *"Do not repay anyone evil for evil. Be careful to do what is right in the eyes of everybody. If it is possible, as far as it depends on you, live at peace with everyone."* The goal is to live at peace with everyone, but sometimes this ideal in not possible. This is why Paul includes two important qualifiers: If it is possible and as far as it depends on you. In a perfect world, it would be easy to live at peace with everyone. However, we don't yet live in that perfect world. Until we do, we have to live with the qualifiers. Our responsibility is to do our best to promote peace and harmony in our relationships. We are responsible before God to maintain our side of the street. But we are not responsible, nor can we be responsible, for maintaining the other person's side of the street.

So, what do we do when our efforts at peace are rebuffed by our critics? Listen to the rest of Paul's advice in Romans 12:19-21. *"Do not take revenge, my friends, but leave room for God's wrath, for it is written: 'It is mine to avenge; I will repay, says the Lord.'"* Again, we see the best way to handle critics is to turn upward.

When criticized, you would do well to remember the old proverb, *"If you wrestle with a pig in the mud, you get dirty and the pig enjoys it!"* Never allow your critics the pleasure of discouraging or distracting you from fulfilling your life purpose. You have to make a choice. Option one: you can turn outward and choose to focus your time and energy into trying to get even with your critics. Option two: you can turn inward and spend your time and energy getting bitter and discouraged by the opposition. Option three: you can turn upward by releasing your critics to God so that you can invest 100 percent of your time and energy into fulfilling your life purpose. You do not have the time and energy to do all three, so you have to choose one.

How do you tend to react when criticized? Do you turn outward (lashing out at those around you, guilty or innocent), inward (storing up anger and grudges), or upward (turning your critics over to God)?

_____

_____

_____

_____

In the New Testament we see the Apostle Paul following the same path as Nehemiah when he faces his critics. Paul has his share of critics throughout his ministry, from Judiazers in Galatia to false teachers in Asia Minor to the Jewish Sanhedrin in Jerusalem. His critics never seem to let up. At the very end of his life, Paul writes a letter to his dear friend, Timothy. He has a special warning for his friend about a particular critic, a man named Alexander. Watch how Paul looks upward as he turns his critic over to God. *"Alexander the metalworker did me a great deal of harm. The Lord will repay him for what he has done. You too should be on your guard against him, because he strongly opposed our message"* (II Timothy 4:14-15). Instead of turning inward or outward, Paul turns upward and turns his critic over to God.

Nehemiah decides to do the same as he turns his critics over to God so that he can focus all of his energies on building the wall. He wisely protects the vision. What is the result of Nehemiah's decision? Nehemiah 4:6 says, *"So we rebuilt the wall till all of it reached half its height, for the people worked with all their heart."* The vision is protected, the work continues and the wall reaches the halfway mark. What a great lesson we learn from Nehemiah. When opposition comes, and it will, protect your vision.

What are some practical things you need to do today to protect your vision?

_____

_____

_____

_____

Protect Your Vulnerable Spots (Nehemiah 4:7-12)

Nehemiah's critics do not give up easily. Listen to how they react when they hear the reports that the work on the wall is continuing. *"But when Sanballat, Tobiah, the Arabs, the Ammonites and the men of Ashdod heard that the repairs to Jerusalem's walls had gone ahead and that the gaps were being closed, they were very angry. They all plotted together to come and fight against Jerusalem and stir up trouble against it"* (vv. 7-8). To fight off their continued attacks, Nehemiah combines prayer and action. He does not waste valuable time picking a fight with his critics. But he is not naive. He takes positive steps to protect his vulnerable spots. *"But we prayed to our God and posted a guard day and night to meet this threat"* (v. 9). Nehemiah would agree with the old Revolutionary War soldiers' saying, "Trust God, but keep the powder dry!"

Nehemiah's critics do not give up easily and neither will your detractors. Therefore, you must be wise and diligent in protecting your vulnerable spots. What are your vulnerable spots? Ridicule, criticism, discouragement, isolation, procrastination, feelings of inferiority? This is no time for vain pride or naivety. What are the weaknesses in your personality where the enemy can penetrate? Everyone has vulnerable spots susceptible to attack. The secret to successfully overcoming them is to admit you have them. You must identify your vulnerable spots and take the necessary actions to protect yourself. Jesus was fond of saying to his followers, "Watch and pray!" This is still good advice for us today.

Did I mention your critics do not give up easily? Neither do Nehemiah's faultfinders. Critics are like pesky flies. Just when you think they are gone, back they come. This time, their criticisms turn to threats. *"Also our enemies said, 'Before they know it or see us, we will be right there among them and will kill them and put an end to the work.' Then the Jews who lived near them came and told us ten times over, 'Wherever you turn, they will attack us'"* (vv. 11-12). At this point, the workers make a serious mistake. They start listening to the voice of their opponents. The result is a demoralized workforce. *"Meanwhile, the people in Judah said, 'The strength of the laborers is giving out, and there is so much rubble that we cannot rebuild the wall'"* (v. 10).

Notice this next barrage of attacks occurs at the halfway point in the project. In fulfilling your life purpose, you can expect to face times of discouragement at the halfway mark. In any project, regardless of the size or scope, the honeymoon comes to an end. The initial excitement of the adventure fades, and the reality and enormity of the task ahead sets in. You and your team are vulnerable at this point in the journey to discouragement, so you must be vigilant. Do not entertain the voice of your opposition. Listen to your critics long enough and you will shift your focus away from your mission and on to the discouraging message of your detractors. This is the mistake made by the workers. All they feel at this point is their strength is giving out and the amount of rubble seems to be growing day by day.

This reminds me of the tragic story of the death of Karl Wallenda. Shortly after this great tightrope walker fell to his death in 1978, his wife recalled, "All Karl thought about for three straight months prior to his fall was falling. It was the first time he'd ever thought about that and it seemed to me that he put all his energy into not falling rather than walking the tightrope." Listening to negative criticism can have the same effect on your life purpose. It can cause a fatal shift in your focus. All you think about is not failing instead of how to finish strong. Do not let ongoing opposition or the natural letdown at the halfway mark cause you to lose your vision or your nerve.

What does Nehemiah do to stop the downward spiral of morale on his team? He immediately takes steps to refocus his team on the power of God and away from the voices of the critics. Listen to his words of warning and faith. Watch how his admonition redirects their thoughts back to their powerful God. *"Don't be afraid of them. Remember the Lord, who is great and awesome"* (v. 14). The problem is clearly one of focus. The workers need their leader to refocus their vision on their great and awesome God, not on the naysayers or the immediate challenges before them.

What is the result of Nehemiah's emergency intervention? *"When our enemies heard that we were aware of their plot and that God had frustrated it, we all returned to the wall, each to his own work"* (v. 15). The result of his action can be summarized in one word: progress. The enemy's cover is blown. Their negative talk is nothing more than empty threats. The work continues because the workers have been encouraged. Here we learn the power of words – positive, true, faith-filled words. Words have the ability to either inflate and empower or deflate and demoralize.

I will never forget my first hot-air balloon ride. I did not realize how much work is involved in getting a hot-air balloon off the ground. First, the balloon has to be unloaded from the trailer and spread out on the ground. Next, the ground crew makes sure all the cords are untangled and properly attached to the basket. The balloon pilot carefully secures the burner in place. Then, the pilot turns on the burner and begins to fill the balloon while several crew members hold open the mouth of the balloon. Finally, the balloon is ready for takeoff. It was quite an endeavor to get the balloon inflated and airborne.

After a fun morning of ballooning, we finally landed. I wondered how long it would take to deflate the balloon. It did not take long for me to get my answer. The pilot reached up, grabbed a small cord and gave it a single pull. This cord was attached to a flap at the top of the balloon. Within seconds the entire balloon collapsed on the ground. What seemed to take forever to inflate was deflated quickly by the pull of a single cord.

The same holds true with the power of words and your life purpose. It will take great effort by you and your team to get your dream off the ground. But it can be easily deflated by the negative criticism of just a few. Don't let this happen to you. Don't let this happen to your team. Develop a plan of protection. When opposition comes, and it will, protect your vulnerable spots.

> What are some of your vulnerable spots that the enemy could use to divert your attention away from your life purpose?
>
> _____
>
> _____
>
> _____
>
> _____

Protect Your Team (Nehemiah 4:16-23)

Nehemiah realizes he must once again get the people working together as a team so they can support each other. He immediately implements a two-fold plan of action. First, he strategically gets his workers away from the discouraging influences of the enemy. Second, he quickly surrounds his workers with the positive influences of God's people. The draining impact of the negative critics is replaced by the positive support of the fellow team members. This sounds like the same advice the Apostle Paul gives in Romans 16:17 when he warns, *"I urge you, brothers, to watch out for those who cause divisions and put obstacles in your way that are contrary to the teachings you have learned. Keep away from them."* In the same way, Nehemiah has to get his workers away from the destructive and deflating influences so that the wall construction project will get back on track.

What is the result of Nehemiah's swift action? The workers come together to protect each other and the work on the wall continues because they are once again working as a united team. Just listen to the unity of purpose, the unselfish support and the mutual protection. *"From that day on, half of my men did the work, while the other half were equipped with spears, shields, bows and armor. The officers posted themselves behind all the people of Judah who were building the wall. Those who carried materials did their work with one hand and held a weapon in the other, and each of the builders wore his sword at his side as he worked. But the man who sounded the trumpet stayed with me"* (vv. 16-18).

What a great plan of action implemented by Nehemiah. Just when his enemies think they are gaining the upper hand, Nehemiah reverses their damaging influence. He does it by making the protection of his team a top priority. A leader will never go wrong by doing whatever it takes to protect his team.

What are some practical ways you can protect your dream team?

_____

_____

_____

_____

_____

_____

We all know Christians who think they don't need the support of fellow believers. The team concept of Christianity is a foreign idea when it comes to their Christian walk. They approach the Christian life as Lone Ranger disciples. This kind of rugged individualism has no place in Christianity because it is doomed to leave the person vulnerable to discouragement and defeat.

They fail to recognize one of the great themes found in Scripture. This theme is found in the one another commands throughout the New Testament: love one another, serve one another, accept one another, forgive one another, greet one another, bear with one another, be devoted to one another, honor one another, teach one another, submit to one another, encourage one another. My question for these solo Christians is always the same: how can you obey any of these commands alone? In order to be obedient to these Biblical commands, a person has to have another on the receiving end.

The Biblical word for this truth is _fellowship_. The Greek word in the New Testament is koinonia, which literally means sharing life together. My favorite definition of fellowship is two fellows in a ship! This is one of God's greatest and most gracious gifts to his people, the gift of fellow travelers on the journey of life. God created us with the need for fellowship and partnership. Don't violate God's plan by attempting to do life alone. Find some good fellows and enjoy fellowship.

Nehemiah is nothing short of brilliant in the way he builds, encourages and protects his team by creating an atmosphere of fellowship. He understands the value of getting his workers together for mutual support and protection. In your journey to find and fulfill your life purpose, you will need a support team. You are not a one-man-show. There are no Lone Ranger Christians. Remember, even the Lone Ranger had Tonto. You will need people to pray for you, advise you and encourage you. Never forget to support your support team. When opposition comes, and it will, protect your team.

It does not matter how noble your life purpose or how committed you are to seeing it fulfilled, you can expect external opposition. Jesus was correct when he said to his disciples, *"In this world you will have trouble"* (John 16:33). The secret to successfully overcoming this kind of opposition is to expect it and develop a plan to overcome it.

The story is told of the day Robert Fulton scheduled the maiden voyage of his steamboat, Clermont. A large crowd gathered to see if this strange new contraption could really work. For several hours the craft belched smoke and sparks from its tall, thin stack as Fulton's engineers attempted to get up the necessary head of steam. When the time finally came to cast off, the boat began to shake and vibrate violently. A group of doubting Thomases in the crowd shouted, "She'll never start! She'll never start!" But Fulton and his crew continued to work. Finally, the boat slowly pulled away from the dock and started to move down the river. After a moment of astonished silence, the voices of the scoffers resumed their ridicule, this time shouting, "She'll never stop! She'll never stop!"[5]

If you are serious about accomplishing your life purpose, get ready for your critics. They may occasionally change their tune, but it's just the same song, second verse. Learn how to tune out the negative critics and tune in to the power of Almighty God. Do whatever it takes to protect your vision, protect your vulnerable spots and protect your team. Nehemiah's plan works. Read the rest of his journal and you will discover the enemies never again mount an armed attack on Nehemiah or his workers. They were all talk and no action. As it ends up they were just full of hot air, kind of like my hot air balloon.

Listen to the words of Theodore Roosevelt in *Citizenship in a Republic*, a speech delivered in Paris, April 23, 1910. The following portion of his speech summarizes what Nehemiah and his team learned at the halfway mark of reaching their goal.

> *It is not the critic who counts; not the man who points out how the strong man stumbles or where the doer of deeds could have done them better. The credit belongs to the man who is actually in the arena, whose face is marred by dust and sweat and blood; who strives valiantly; who errs, and comes up short again and again, because there is no effort without error and shortcoming; but who does actually try to do the deeds; who knows the great enthusiasms, the great devotions, who spends himself in a worthy cause; who at the best knows in the end the triumph of high achievement, and who at the worst, if he fails, at least fails while daring greatly, so that his place shall never be with those cold and timid souls who know neither victory nor defeat.[6]*

What are some practical steps that you and your dream team can take to remain in the arena of dust and sweat and blood daring mighty things?

_____

_____

_____

_____

_____

_____

_____

Living My Dash: Overcoming External Opposition

In May of 1998, the initial stage of my vision to plant a purpose-driven church in Roswell had become a reality. With over 400 charter members, we were off to a great start. We were excited to have the Roswell Civic Center as our new home. Many churches would be envious of the beautiful and spacious facilities we enjoyed for our first four years. But there was a problem: in a small town, people don't consider a church to be a real church unless it has a building. Church plants in large cities can often meet for decades in rented facilities and still be considered a legitimate church. However, people in small towns think differently than big city folks. A church is considered a temporary church until it occupies its own building. I had numerous people assure me that once we got a real church building, they would be joining us. I thought at the time how odd, but now I know they were telling me the truth. Four years later they showed up for the first Sunday service in our new building.

We soon encountered another problem in our temporary facility: weekend conventions. Hosting weekend conventions was understandably the top priority of the Civic Center. We understood this from the beginning. When a weekend convention was scheduled in the Civic Center, it meant we had to find another location for that weekend. This was no easy task in a facility-challenged community like Roswell. Most of these Sundays were spent under the shade trees at a local park. We advertised these Sunday assemblies as Church in the Park Sundays. Privately, I called them *Pray for no rain Sundays*. When we had to meet elsewhere during the winter months, we would meet at the local college campus where we rented their Performing Arts Center. We tried to make the best of our church-on-the-move situation. I still remember one of our advertising slogans in the local newspaper: Only intelligent people attend Grace Community Church – they have to be smart enough to find us on Sundays!

These were still exciting days, even though we got tired of the weekly set-up and tear-down routine. Being a porta-church is hard work and at times is not that inviting to visitors. However, new people continued to come every week to check us out. A good number of these guests were families with children and teenagers. This created another problem. We were limited in space for children and youth ministries. Civic Centers are not designed with Christian ministries in mind. There were a few small meeting rooms attached to the main auditorium, but we quickly maxed out these makeshift classrooms. Our nursery was overflowing, which is not something a visiting mother wants for her baby. We desperately needed a permanent home. We had to find property and build our own building... soon.

Our building team was on the lookout for a piece of property that would not only meet our needs, but also fit in our price range. We found a beautiful 22 acre piece of property that would be perfect for our future church home. It was located in a developing residential neighborhood in a good section of the city with a city park next door. Most importantly, it was priced to sell. We made an offer and it was accepted. I could not believe how smoothly the purchase transpired. It was clearly a God thing. The entire purchasing process had God's fingerprints all over it. I thought everything was working perfectly until I received a phone call from the building team leader. There was a problem. This was not a no-big-deal size problem; this was a *Houston-we've-got-a-problem* size problem. I could not believe what I was hearing. Our future neighbors were objecting to having a church in their neighborhood.

I couldn't imagine anyone would oppose a church being built in their neighborhood. I could understand the objections if someone were building a pig farm or a bar in their neighborhood. But a church? Why would anyone be opposed to a church? Over the next few months I discovered the reason for their opposition. They actually had a written list of objections they presented to city officials. I am still baffled at the inexplicable reasons given for their protest. *"Our property values will drop like a rock; our houses will be flooded with rain water running off the church parking lots; they will build large, ugly metal buildings; big yellow buses will be parked out front; horrible traffic jams will block our streets every Sunday; bright parking lot lights will flood our bedroom windows all night; loud Christian rock music will shake the walls of our homes!"*

The negative neighbors were few in number, but persistent and loud in their attack. They hired an attorney to present their case and opposed us at city hall. Eventually they took the case all the way to district court. The church members reacted to the opposition in a variety of ways. Some turned inward and became discouraged. They saw the external opposition as a sign that we should look for another piece of property. After all, why should we move into this particular neighborhood if the neighbors didn't want us there? They saw the conflict as a foreboding of more conflicts for years to come.

Other members reacted outwardly and prepared for a fight. They readied themselves for battle, confident God was on our side against the unbelieving Philistine neighbors. Some of these members would arrive at the city council meetings with scowls on their faces, looking more like a lynch mob than a church. I appreciated their passion, even if it was misdirected. I found it to be quite a challenge to bring peace and calm to this group, encouraging them to be kind and loving, and allow the legal process time to work.

The biggest challenge for me as a leader throughout this experience was to encourage the church members to turn upward. I realized this would be a great opportunity to teach this principle. Just like Nehemiah, I knew if they could learn to trust God in this challenging moment, they would be well prepared to face other battles certain to come in the future. So I continually reminded them of our great and awesome God who was in total control of our situation. We didn't need to retreat in fear or attack in anger. We just needed to be Christ-like and trust God with the process. I reminded them of Jesus' admonition to love your enemies and do good to those who persecute you and say all manner of evil against you. As I look back now on this difficult period in our church's history, I can now see how this crisis ended up being a great spiritual growth experience for our church family.

The negative neighbors eventually lost their court battle. We were able to purchase the land and eventually build our new worship center, but not without a cost in time and legal fees. Just so you will know the rest of the story, the property values have actually increased in the neighborhood, no houses have been flooded by water running off of the church parking lots, there are no big yellow buses out front, no ugly metal buildings have been built on our property and the parking lot lights go out at 10:00 o'clock every evening.

We have tried to go out of our way to be good neighbors. We even built one negative neighbor a new fence in his backyard at our expense so he wouldn't have to look at our property. Our campus has been beautifully landscaped with hundreds of trees, flowers and shrubs. I was pleasantly surprised one day several years after the court battle ended when one of the most vocal neighbors told us she loved what we had done to the property. In fact, our campus has received the city's beautification award... twice. I guess Jesus was right again; it pays to go the second mile, even with ornery folks. I will have to throw our critics one bone. There are Sunday morning traffic jams, but they don't last too long. Now here's the best news of all, several of our neighbors are now attending our church.

In your journey to find and fulfill your life purpose, you can expect opposition from your ornery catfish. Moses had his Pharaoh, Joshua had his Philistines, Jesus had his Pharisees, Paul had his Judaizers, Nehemiah had his Sanballat and we had our neighbors. Guess what? You will have your share of critics, too.

You must not let them discourage or distract you from living your dash. Protect your vision, protect your vulnerable spots and protect your team. Do this and you will be well on your way to finding and fulfilling your life purpose.

Living Your Dash

CHAPTER 3 – OVERCOME EXTERNAL OPPOSITION

Step #1: Protect Your Vision (Nehemiah 4:1-5)
I anticipate that some people will be opposed to the vision God has given me for my life purpose. Rather than turning inwardly with hostility or outwardly with anger, I choose to turn upwardly to God for strength of resolve and clarity of vision.

Step #2: Protect Your Vulnerable Spots (Nehemiah 4:7-12)
Just as I have strengths, I also have weaknesses. Rather than trying to hide these vulnerabilities from God, I openly acknowledge them and ask God for the strength and wisdom to protect me from the enemy's attack.

Step #3: Protect Your Team (Nehemiah 4:16-23)
My dream team and I are better together. We will work together as a team to accomplish God's purpose for our lives. We will protect one another through accountability and prayer, not allowing the enemy to gain a foothold.

Father God,

You taught me that if you are for me, who can stand against me? You also made it clear that the world would be in opposition to your plans. Therefore, Lord, help me not to be surprised by opposition, but to welcome it as an opportunity to demonstrate faith and resolve. Show me my areas of vulnerability and help me work together with my dream team to overcome them. Let me be as committed to helping others fulfill their life purpose as I am to fulfilling my own.

In Jesus name I pray, Amen.

OVERCOME
INTERNAL CONFLICTS

*The first and last task of a leader is to keep hope alive – the hope that we can
finally find our way through to a better world – despite the day's actions, despite
our own inertness and shallowness and wavering resolve.*
John W. Gardner

Out of every crisis comes a chance to be reborn.
Nena O'Neill

One evening as I was channel surfing, I came across an interesting documenta-
ry on the History Channel. It was a video showing a lion attacking its prey. I
learned the king of the jungle has a predictable routine when he attacks. He
carefully sneaks up on the unsuspecting herd and then attacks. But the lion's goal is not to
kill the entire herd. He's not that hungry or stupid. His desire is to separate one member
from the rest of the herd. His strategy is simple: divide and conquer. Once the lion is
able to successfully separate his victim from the rest of the herd, it's just a matter of time
before dinner is served.

Divide and conquer. This strategy is as old as the Garden of Eden. You do remember
how the tempting Serpent caught Eve while she was alone. The Apostle Peter describes
this time-tested strategy of Satan in similar terms and how he uses it when attacking
Christians. *"Your enemy the devil prowls around like a roaring lion looking for someone to devour"* (I
Peter 5:8). Just like a lion in search of its prey, the devil uses the divide-and-conquer strategy on Christians. We see it in the betrayal of Jesus in the Gospels. When Satan attacks
Jesus' original team of the Twelve Apostles, notice he does not go after all 12 at once. He
carefully and strategically isolates Judas from the rest of the team. Once Judas is separated, he is vulnerable and becomes an easy target for Satan. The description of the events
during the Last Supper in John's Gospel is sobering. *"As soon as Judas took the bread, Satan
entered into him… As soon as Judas had taken the bread, he went out. And it was night"* (John

13:27,30).

The enemy's goal is the same today in his desire to prevent you from doing a great work for God. He wants to either isolate you from the rest of your support team or he wants to create isolation within your team. One of the primary ways Satan loves to get a Christian separated and isolated from other Christians is by creating internal conflicts. If Satan can get Christians fighting and attacking each other, he knows this will increase his chances of derailing their life missions by using his divide-and-conquer tactic. Once the Devil convinces one team member that the real enemy is another team member, suddenly the crosshairs are no longer on him as the primary adversary. He has then successfully deflected the attention off of himself and onto someone else.

This very scenario is the next big challenge Nehemiah faces in his life purpose quest. With the construction of the wall just past the halfway point, Nehemiah is suddenly confronted with a major problem. This challenge has the potential to derail the entire project and interrupt Nehemiah's life purpose. The problem is described in the first part of chapter five. A famine has caused a shortage of food in the land of Israel. These dire circumstances force the poor to borrow money from the rich just to purchase the necessities of life. They have no other alternative except to secure their loans by putting up as collateral their land, possessions and even their children. The wealthy citizens are more than happy to loan their fellow Jews the money needed to survive. However, this action develops into a major problem. The wealthy Jews begin to take advantage of the situation by charging their poor Jewish neighbors usury or excessive interest.

The practice of usury between Jews is strictly forbidden in the Law of Moses. Moses explicitly commanded the Jewish people entering the Promised Land, *"Do not charge your brother interest, whether on money or food or anything else that may earn interest"* (Deuteronomy 23:19). The command is clear, but the Jews in Jerusalem are blatantly disobeying God's law by charging interest on their loans to their fellow Jews. When the poor cannot pay the bill on their loans, the wealthy are foreclosing on their fellow Jews, taking their land and possessions, and even taking their children as slaves. It is a classic case of the haves abusing the have-nots. Finally the have-nots have enough of the abuse and verbalize their protest to Nehemiah.

Nehemiah describes their frustration in his journal. *"Now the men and their wives raised a great outcry against their Jewish brothers. Some were saying, 'We and our sons and daughters are numerous; in order for us to stay alive, we must get grain.' Others were saying, 'We are mortgaging our fields, our vineyards and our homes to get grain during the famine.' Still others were saying, 'We have to pay the king's tax on our fields and vineyards. Although we are of the same flesh and blood as our countrymen and though our sons are as good as theirs, yet we have to subject our sons and daughters to slavery. Some of our daughters have already been enslaved, but we are powerless, because our fields and our vineyards belong to others'"* (5:1-5).

What a mess. Just when things are going well and the external opposition of the enemies has been thwarted, suddenly there is a new problem. To everyone's surprise, there is internal conflict. That's how it often happens with internal conflicts. You don't see it coming. Just when things are looking up and progress is being made, out of nowhere comes internal conflict. Nothing can drain the joy and motivation out of a leader like waking up to discover internal conflict in the camp.

How will Nehemiah handle this challenge affecting his team? These are the very people who have faithfully served him during this building project. They have worked hard and worked together to build the wall. Nehemiah knows them by name and counts them as friends and partners in this great work of God. But now their unity is in jeopardy, not because of outside opposition, but because of internal division. There is separation and division on his team. How will Nehemiah navigate the land mines of internal conflict?

The rest of chapter five describes how Nehemiah addresses the problem of internal conflict. As a leader, you need to learn this lesson if you hope to fulfill your life purpose because, like it or not, you will have internal conflicts on your team. They are as unavoidable as death and taxes. You must learn how to handle these conflicts in a positive and strategic way. Otherwise, you and your team will be vulnerable to Satan's divide-and-conquer strategy, and your life purpose can easily be derailed. It's now time to get out your pen and notebook again, and get ready to take extensive notes from this master leader. From Nehemiah's example, you are about to learn how to overcome internal conflict when it attacks your team.

Recall a time when you have observed a team (family, church, business, etc.) struggle with internal conflict? What was the result?

_____

_____

_____

_____

Consider the Conflict (Nehemiah 5:1-7)

How does Nehemiah respond when he initially hears the complaint? This is extremely important because this is where many leaders make a critical mistake. Nehemiah listens to the charges and then "ponders them in his mind" (v. 7). Don't move too quickly over this phrase. When a wise leader hears the early rumblings of an internal conflict, his first response is to ponder what he has heard. This means the leader must take time to give serious consideration to the report. Responding in this way is not easy for most leaders because they want to focus on the project to be completed, not the personal conflicts between team members. This is why leaders don't like internal conflicts. They want to spend their time building the wall, not conducting counseling sessions.

Leaders can easily do a nosedive here if they are not careful, especially if they have a tendency to rush to judgment in order to avoid dealing with conflicts on the team. This problem is intensified by the fact that leaders are drawn toward action, not inaction. They don't like to sit around and talk an issue to death. This natural tendency to make decisions quickly can cause a leader to act before all the facts have been carefully examined. If sufficient time and attention are not given to a team member's feelings of mistreatment, great damage can be done to the unity of the team. Wise leaders know the value of this kind of pondering, especially when the issue is one of internal conflict.

> Anytime there is a struggle within an organization, the leader must respond.

I have to confess that I learned this lesson the hard way. As a young leader, I had a tendency to react too quickly when I got wind of an internal conflict. I found myself tempted to take the side of the first person reporting the conflict. Over the years, however, I have learned there are always two sides to every story. Actually, there are always three sides to every story: his side, her side and what actually happened. It is the practice of the wise leader to get all three sides of the story when evaluating an internal conflict.

Anytime there is a struggle within an organization, the leader must respond. There are basically three ways for a leader to handle the news of a potential internal conflict. My guess is that you will find yourself falling neatly into one of these three categories.

First, a leader can *dismiss the conflict* by concluding, "This is no big deal; they are making a mountain out of a mole hill." Any experienced leader knows that every reported crisis is not automatically a true crisis. But to simply dismiss the report is inviting disaster. Leaders must face the fact that in a fallen world, legitimate conflicts are a natural result of people working together. When leaders are quick to dismiss a conflict, they are in effect dismissing the person voicing the concern. To ignore a charge is to devalue a member of the team and puts out the welcome mat for additional conflict.

Second, a leader can *deny the conflict* by saying, "If I pretend there is no conflict, I'm sure it will disappear. Time heals all wounds, so let's do nothing." Certainly there are occasions when allowing tempers to cool down can help bring calm to the storm. However, a wise leader will be the first to admit that time does not automatically heal all wounds. In fact, burying your head in the sand seldom solves anything and greatly weakens the leader's influence in an organization. People want to believe their leaders are intelligent enough to see legitimate conflicts and have the courage to deal with these conflicts in a healthy manner. More often than not, delaying a response simply allows the wound to fester and get worse.

Third, a leader can *deal with the conflict*. This is the option Nehemiah selects. He listens to the complaint and gives it serious consideration. He investigates the complaint to find out all the facts and the seriousness of the problem. Before he decides on his response, he wants to hear all three sides of the story. This is the only healthy response to an internal conflict because it actually deals with the problem. Nehemiah demonstrates great wisdom and first-class leadership skills in dealing honestly and directly with this internal conflict.

Most leaders have a natural default tendency to one of these three responses. When confronted with an internal conflict, they will decide to dismiss it, deny it or deal with it. Which of the three is your natural default tendency? Maybe your personality is like mine. I never met a conflict I did not want to avoid. I have a natural propensity to either dismiss or deny conflicts. I want everyone on my team to be nice, get along with each other and stay focused on the big target. But I have learned an important law of leadership: conflict is a natural and unavoidable part of the life purpose journey of a leader. Whether you love or hate confrontation is not the issue. The question is, "Do you as a leader have the courage to confront the problem of internal conflict when it arises on your team?"

Generally speaking, the longer a leader postpones dealing with an internal conflict, the worse it becomes. Internal conflict on a team is like a bacterial infection. It seldom heals on its own. The longer you wait to take antibiotics, the worse the infection becomes. On a team, the infection tends to not only intensify with the concerned parties, but it also starts infecting other team members because people have a natural tendency to take sides in a conflict.

Nehemiah's response is impressive and effective. He does not bury his head in the sand, pretending the problem is not legitimate. The complaint proves to be valid and the abuse is inexcusable. He cannot dismiss it. Neither does he try to wish away the conflict, hoping the conflict will either disappear or repair itself. This conflict will not be resolved without strong leadership on his part. Nehemiah wisely decides to deal with the conflict in a healthy and redemptive way so that in the end it becomes a win-win solution for all involved.

Like Nehemiah, you must be careful to not fall into the trap of dismissing or denying the reality of internal conflicts. As difficult as it may be, deal with them. When internal conflicts arise, and they will, you must consider the conflict.

What is your default tendency with internal conflict (dismiss it, deny it, or deal with it)?

_____

_____

_____

_____

What changes could you make to improve the way you deal with conflict?

_____

_____

_____

_____

_____

Confront the Conflict (Nehemiah 5:7-8)

Nehemiah takes sufficient time to consider the complaint and learns the allegation is legitimate. The wealthy Jews are taking advantage of their less fortunate Jewish neighbors. Now Nehemiah is ready to act. His response can be summarized in one word: anger. Listen to his response in his own words. *"When I heard their outcry and these charges, I was very angry. I pondered them in my mind and then accused the nobles and officials. I told them, 'You are exacting usury from your own countrymen!'"* (vv. 6-7). Nehemiah does not mince words with the wealthy. Their behavior is nothing short of reprehensible and it must come to a screeching halt. *"What you are doing is not right. Shouldn't you walk in the fear of our God to avoid the reproach of our Gentile enemies?"* (v. 9).

Nehemiah has worked hard to purchase all the Jews owned by their Gentile neighbors. Now these wealthy nobles and officials are undoing his liberating work. It is no wonder Nehemiah is fuming mad. His argument is convincing and convicting. The wealthy Jews are speechless. *"They kept quiet, because they could find nothing to say"* (v. 8). Here we see a great leader and man of God get angry. Read his words again. *"I was very angry."* This part of Nehemiah's story may surprise and shock some people. Is it proper for a godly leader to get angry?

Where did we ever get the idea that Christians should never get angry? We certainly did not get it from the Bible. For example, the Gospels are very clear that Jesus got angry. Do you remember Jesus confronting the Jewish leaders in Matthew 23? Listen to his stinging rebuke. *"Woe to you, teachers of the law and Pharisees, you hypocrites! You clean the outside of the cup and dish, but inside they are full of greed and self-indulgence. Blind Pharisee! First clean the inside of the cup and dish, and then the outside also will be clean. Woe to you, teachers of the law and Pharisees, you hypocrites! You are like white-washed tombs, which look beautiful on the outside but on the inside are full of dead men's bones and everything unclean. In the same way, on the outside you appear to people as righteous but on the inside you are full of hypocrisy and wickedness"* (Matthew 23:25-28). This doesn't sound like a man trying to win friends and influence people. Jesus was angry.

Remember also the violent cleansing of the temple by Jesus. What would cause the meek-and-mild Jesus to react so violently? The same reason Nehemiah reacted with such force. The Jewish leaders in Jesus' day were also abusing their Jewish brothers. The wealthy Sadducees, who controlled the priesthood and temple organization, were ripping the people off in three ways.

First, they had a practice of routinely rejecting the sacrificial animals brought by the Jewish people to the temple to be offered to God. The priests could always find some flaw in the animal. However, the greedy priests had the perfect solution. They just so happened to have temple-approved sacrificial animals on sale. Of course, these animals were on sale at an inflated price. The worshipers were caught between a rock and a hard place. The only way they could offer their sacrifices was to purchase the pre-approved animals from the temple priests at the bloated price. So the temple priests were getting rich by overcharging the Jewish pilgrims for their officially sanctioned sacrificial animals.

Second, the priests were gouging the Jewish pilgrims with exorbitant money exchange fees for their offerings. Roman coins were not acceptable as a temple offering. But again, the priests had the perfect solution. They would gladly exchange the evil Roman coins for kosher Jewish coins. Or course, there would be a handling fee added to the transaction. Once again, the worshipers were being ripped off by the religious establishment. This made Jesus so angry that he made a whip out of cords, drove out of the temple those who were buying and selling the animals and overturned the tables of the money changers. It is no exaggeration when Jesus accused these leaders of turning the temple of God into "a den of robbers" (Mark 11:17).

Third, the Sadducees were allowing people to carry merchandise through the temple courts. More than likely, this was happening in the area known as the Court of the Gentiles. This part of the temple courts was specifically set aside for Gentiles to come and worship the true and living God. But the temple authorities were allowing their area of worship to become a short-cut through the temple grounds. Can you imagine trying to worship God in this flea market atmosphere? Jesus reacted strongly to this abuse of the Gentile worshipers and would not allow anyone to carry merchandise through the temple courts. He did this because he passionately loved all people, even the Gentiles. He believed the temple was not just for the Jews. It was also to be a *"house of prayer for all nations"* (Mark 11:17).

Jesus is the perfect example of how and when to get angry. God's people, especially God's leaders, must realize that sometimes it is a sin not to get angry, particularly when innocent and vulnerable people are being abused. The secret is to channel anger in a positive direction to stop the abuse. The purpose of anger is never to vent personal frustration or to get some kind of secret pleasure in blowing up. Read the end of Matthew 23 and you will see the motivation behind Jesus' anger. He is not enjoying his rebuke of the Jewish leaders. It is breaking his heart to see their self-righteous attitude and actions. *"O Jerusalem, Jerusalem, you who kill the prophets and stone those sent to you, how often I have longed to gather your children together, as a hen gathers her chicks under her wings, but you were not willing"* (Matthew

> Like Jesus, Nehemiah channels his frustration like a surgeon using a scalpel to remove a cancerous tumor.

23:37). Jesus found no pleasure in reprimanding the Jewish leaders, but he knew the abuse had to be exposed. So he channeled his anger to reveal the sin.

Like Jesus, Nehemiah channels his frustration like a surgeon using a scalpel to remove a cancerous tumor. Channeled anger is a powerful tool to bring about positive change. A great modern-day example of this good kind of anger is the organization MADD. Mothers Against Drunk Driving is an organization comprised of people who do more than just get angry. They channel and direct their anger like a laser beam to pass legislation to get drunk drivers off the road. Thousands of lives have been saved because a group of grieving mothers decided it was time to get angry.

The Apostle Paul warns, *"In your anger do not sin. Do not let the sun go down while you are still angry and do not give the devil a foothold"* (Ephesians 4:26-27). Listen carefully to his words. He never says, "Christians, don't get angry." He simply teaches Christ followers how to avoid sinning when they get angry. In other words, don't let the sun go down before you deal with the anger in a positive and constructive way. The secret to successfully navigating internal conflict is controlled anger. Deal with conflicts before they have time to grow and spread. When internal conflicts arise, and they will, confront the conflict.

What internal conflict(s) are you experiencing as you seek to fulfill your life purpose?

_____

_____

_____

_____

How have you responded proactively to anger rather than reactively?

_____

_____

_____

_____

_____

Correct the Conflict (Nehemiah 5:9-19)

Simply confronting the problem, however, does not necessarily solve the conflict. There needs to be a positive solution offered. Most anyone can identify a problem, but it takes a master leader to devise a positive plan to solve the problem. The ultimate goal is to address the conflict in a redemptive way that not only solves the problem but also restores the relationships of the people involved and hopefully repairs any damage done by the conflict. This is a tall order for any leader, but Nehemiah is wise enough to understand the delicate balance of confronting and correcting. His next move is to correct the problem with two specific actions.

First, he prescribes a plan. His plan is simple, clear and measurable. The nobles and officials must agree to stop the abusive practices of usury and immediately return the foreclosed land and possessions. In addition, they must agree to free the enslaved children. Notice how he begins his plea in verse nine by calling on the Jewish nobles and officials to do what is right in God's eyes. *"So I continued, 'What you are doing is not right. Shouldn't you walk in the fear of our God to avoid the reproach of our Gentile enemies?"'*

Nehemiah wants them to do the right thing, but he wants them to do it for the right reason, namely out of fear and reverence for their God. Correcting their bad behavior just because they got caught is not good enough for Nehemiah. He knows that a deeper motivation is necessary for lasting transformation.

Second, he models the plan. Nehemiah does not just proclaim, "Here's what I want you to do!" Instead, he says, "Watch me; here is how I want you to do it." Nehemiah is not a do as I say, not as I do kind of leader. He knows talk is cheap and actions speak louder than words. He decides to lead by example in very specific and concrete ways. To begin with, he and his men have been helping the poor by lending them money, but they have been very careful not to charge them interest. This gives Nehemiah the moral integrity and clout to order the nobles and officials to *"let the exacting of usury stop!"* (v. 10). Had he been violating the usury law himself, his words would have been hollow.

If you recall, Nehemiah is the official governor of Judah, having been appointed to the position by King Artaxerxes. This political position provides him with a number of perks. The governors before Nehemiah had taken advantage of these benefits and abused the people by placing heavy taxes on them and requiring them to contribute food and wine for the governor. However, Nehemiah refused to take advantage of his political position. He is quick to remind the nobles and officials of this fact. *"Moreover, from the twentieth year of King Artaxerxes, when I was appointed to be their governor in the land of Judah, until his thirty-second year – twelve years – neither I nor my brothers ate the food allotted to the governor"* (v. 14). Nehemiah had refused for his entire 12 year term as governor to be the kind of leader that *"lorded it over the people"* (v. 15). That is leading by example and doing it for a long time. This is the kind of behavior that will fill the credibility bucket of a leader.

The good news is Nehemiah gets buy-in from everyone involved. The wealthy Jews agree to Nehemiah's plan. *"We will give it back,"* they said. *"And we will not demand anything more from them. We will do as you say"* (v.12). It is difficult to argue in the face of this kind of unswerving integrity.

Nothing will destroy the integrity of your life purpose as much as inconsistency. There must be harmony between your walk and your talk. Lead with your behavior, not your mouth. A wise leader leads by personal example and with steadfast integrity. Do not be like the lady who was angry because someone broke into her home and stole her favorite Holiday Inn towels.

Like Nehemiah, you must practice what you preach by modeling the desired behavior. Don't be like the identical twin brothers who lived in the same town. One was a pastor and the other was a physician. One Monday morning, the doctor passed a lady on the sidewalk. She said to the doctor, "Pastor, the sermon you preached yesterday was wonderful." The doctor protested, "I'm sorry, Madam, but you have me confused with my brother. You see, he preaches and I practice!"

A wise leader will follow the instructions of the Apostle John in his first letter. *"This is how we know what love is: Jesus Christ laid down his life for us. And we ought to lay down our lives for our brothers. If anyone has material possessions and sees his brother in need but has no pity on him, how can the love of God be in him? Dear children, let us not love with words or tongue but with actions and truth"* (I John 3:16-18).

Why does Nehemiah demonstrate this kind of love for his brothers and sisters in need? What is the underlying incentive for his sacrificial actions? His motivation is two-fold. First, he acts out of reverence for God. Even though previous governors ate the food allotted to the governor and placed a heavy burden on the people with excessive taxes, Nehemiah does not follow their example. *"But out of reverence for God I did not act like that"* (v.15). Nehemiah knows he will have to someday answer to God for the way he treats his fellow man. His deep respect for God motivates and inspires his servant leadership.

Second, he acts out of love for his people. Nehemiah has every right as the governor to enjoy the perks of his office. But he refuses. *"I never demanded the food allotted to the governor, because the demands were heavy on the people"* (v.18). Nehemiah seems to be guided by one overriding principle: people matter to God, so they matter to him. He genuinely cares about these struggling Jews trying to rebuild their homeland. He wants them to succeed and is willing to sacrifice whatever it takes to help them reach their goal.

This is true servant leadership, the kind of leadership Jesus promoted and practiced. *"You know that those who are regarded as rulers of the Gentiles lord it over them, and their high officials exercise authority over them. Not so with you. Instead, whoever wants to become great among you must be your servant, and whoever wants to be first must be slave of all. For even the Son of Man did not come to be served, but to serve, and to give his life as a ransom for many"* (Mark 10:42-45).

The story is told of a man who fell into a pit and could not get himself out. A subjective person came along and said, "I feel for you down there." An objective person came along and said, "It's logical that someone would fall down there." A Pharisee came along and said, "Only bad people fall into a pit." A mathematician came along and said, "I can calculate how you fell into the pit." A news reporter said, "I want the exclusive story on your fall into the pit." A geologist said, "You should appreciate the rock strata of the pit." The county inspector said, "Do you have a permit for that pit?" A self-pitying person said, "You haven't seen anything until you see my pit!" An optimist said, "Things could be worse!" A pessimist said, "Things will get worse!" But Jesus, seeing the man in the pit, took him by the hand and lifted him out of the pit.

At this crucial moment in Nehemiah's life purpose journey, he demonstrates true leadership and true love. He is facing a conflict that could have derailed the construction of the wall. This internal conflict on his team could have turned into a civil war, dividing the haves and the have-nots. But through wise, servant leadership, Nehemiah helps the people navigate a dangerous passage on the way to fulfilling their dream. Follow Nehemiah's example. This is the way to deal positively with conflict. When internal conflicts arise, and they will, you must be ready and willing with the courage and wisdom of Nehemiah to consider, confront and correct the conflict.

What is your plan to overcome the internal conflict you are experiencing?

_____

_____

_____

_____

Living My Dash: Overcoming Internal Conflict

One of the toughest challenges I faced in planting the new church was the issue of conflicting visions. When people come together to start a new congregation, they each have their own preconceived idea of the kind of church they want to plant. The old saying is true about Christians: Where two or three are gathered together, there are at least four opinions! This was certainly the case in the early stages of our new church plant. Different people had different visions and these differences became the seedbed for internal conflict.

One of my first indications of the challenge before me was the day we named the church. I did not want to be a controlling pastor who made every decision. I wanted the members to have ownership from day one. I thought, "What better way to communicate this goal than to let the members come up with the name." I honestly thought this would be a fun experience for everyone and that, in the end, we would unanimously cheer for the selected name.

I distributed index cards one Sunday morning during the service and asked the people to prayerfully consider an appropriate name for the church, write their suggestions on the index cards and return the cards the next Sunday. I explained how important it was to select a name that connected to unchurched people in our community since they were our primary target. I also explained that it needed to reflect the unique ministry we hoped to have in our city. I passed out the cards, hoping for the best.

Looking back, I must admit I was a bit naïve about this process. I sincerely wanted to get input on the name selection, but I was not ready for what I read on the index cards the next week. I could not believe the suggestions, some of which were strange to say the least. I began to wonder what planet some of these people were from. I honestly thought a jokester slipped in a few weird recommendations as a prank, but I soon discovered that the odd proposals were legitimately submitted. I now wish I had saved this stack of cards, especially the ones with the bizarre suggestions. I could probably find humor in the crazy names today. I think I must have destroyed the cards, subconsciously fearing they might escape my file, go public and someday get attached to a church building. I would never be able to forgive myself.

Thankfully, the voting process over the next few weeks narrowed the choice to several good options and *Grace Community Church* was the final decision. However, I received a subtle warning in this process. I could see a wide variety of pet theological doctrines echoing in some of the suggestions. My spiritual antennae went up when I read potential church names which included words like *First Pentecostal Church of... Roswell Holiness Church of... Roswell Calvinist Church...* and the list went on. I could see a multitude of visions reflected on those index cards and I knew this could lead to internal conflict.

I do not remember where I first heard this tidbit of wisdom, but I have been comforted and guided by it many times: *In planting a church, you will not finish with the same group you begin with.* I have discovered that some people are great starters, but lousy finishers. When a new church is being established, starter Christians come out of the woodwork. They certainly appeared out of nowhere in our early days. I had never seen some of these people and I had lived in this community for over 20 years. But they showed up within the first month of our church plant.

I must admit it was exciting just to have warm bodies showing up to fill the chairs in those first few months. Seeing a full auditorium on Sunday mornings certainly added to the excitement of the new church. However, my excitement was short-lived. I soon learned that starter Christians come with an agenda and a price. Their goal is often to mold the new church into their own image. They quickly make their vision clear: This is the way God and I want this new church to go. When other people offer conflicting visions, the sparks begin to fly and internal conflicts arise. It was at this point in the journey that I discovered another great truth that needs to be added to the church-planting rule book: When starter Christians don't get their way, they leave. Whatever you do, let them leave!

Thankfully, I learned from the example of Nehemiah how to consider, confront and correct internal conflicts. I would love to say all those early conflicts were successfully corrected and everyone lived happily ever after, but church planting and fairy tales have little in common. However, I can say that following Nehemiah's model for conflict resolution worked. Some of the starter Christians actually caught the vision cast by the leadership of the church and are still with us today. Others eventually became frustrated when their vision was not adopted and never returned, an experience I like to call growth by subtraction!

The familiar poem will prove true when it comes to your life purpose:

To dwell above with saints we love,

Oh, that will be glory.

But to dwell below with saints we know,

Well now, that's a different story!

In your journey to find and fulfill your life purpose, you can expect internal conflicts with some of the saints on your team. During this period of time, Satan will be waiting in the bushes, ready to take advantage of the conflicts. Like a lion stalking its prey, the devil will try to use these internal conflicts to divide and conquer.

The internal conflict experienced by Nehemiah could have easily wrecked his life purpose. If he had failed to address the conflict, it could have quickly escalated and the work on the wall could have come to a screeching halt. The same could have been true in the formative days of our church plant, causing the wheels to fall off the bus within the first few months. Believe me when I say a similar experience can happen with your life purpose if you fail to address and overcome internal conflict.

The challenge is the same today when you face internal conflict, so follow the example of Nehemiah: consider it, confront it and then correct it. Overcome the challenge of internal conflict and you will be well on your way to living your dash.

Living Your Dash

CHAPTER 4 – OVERCOME INTERNAL CONFLICTS

Step #1: Consider the Conflict (Nehemiah 5:1-7)
I will deal with conflict as it arises rather than dismissing or denying it. I understand that not dealing with conflict only allows it to escalate and grow.

Step #2: Confront the Conflict (Nehemiah 5:7-8)
In confronting conflict, I will control my anger by channeling it toward a positive outcome.

Step #3: Correct the Conflict (Nehemiah 5:9-19)
When internal conflict threatens my life purpose, I will formulate a plan, refocus on the vision, and be motivated by reverence for God and love for others.

Father God,

The Bible teaches that you did not give me a spirit of fear, but of power, love, and sound mind. Please, grant me the courage to deal with conflict as it arises and the wisdom to resolve it in a way that honors you. Just as Jesus set an example of how to be angry and not sin, teach me to control my anger in the midst of conflict. Lord, help me to be motivated in all I do by reverence for you and love for others.

In Jesus name I pray, Amen.

CHAPTER FIVE

DON'T QUIT
BEFORE THE FINISH LINE

The great majority of men are bundles of beginnings.
Ralph Waldo Emerson

Great works are performed not by strength, but by perseverance.
Samuel Johnson

What do the following share in common: a partially mowed lawn, a half-read book, an unfinished letter, an abandoned diet and a car up on blocks? Answer: they are all projects begun, but never finished.

What is true of lawns, books, letters, diets and cars is also be true of living your dash. It is easy to begin the journey of finding and fulfilling your life mission with a bang, but soon lose the enthusiasm required to complete the job. The honeymoon of new beginnings eventually turns into the daily grind and starts to resemble hard work. You can't pinpoint the day it happened, but one day you woke up and realized the new car smell of your life mission was gone. Words like new, fresh, exciting, adventure are deleted from your vocabulary. This is when you start looking for a towel to throw in so you can quit. There is a human tendency in all of us to quit too soon, to stop before the finish line.

Any good track coach will tell you that successful runners are trained to run through the finish line. They don't run to the finish line; they run through the finish line. Can you imagine a runner slowing down as the finish line approaches and coming to a complete stop the moment he touches the tape? Can you visualize a NASCAR driver letting off of the accelerator during the final turn of the final lap so that he can come to a complete stop immediately after crossing the finish line? There is a name for runners and drivers who finish a race in this fashion – losers.

On March 6, 1987, Eamon Coglan, the Irish world record holder at 1,500 meters, was running in a qualifying heat at the World Indoor Track Championships in Indianapolis. With two and a half laps left in the race, he was tripped. He fell, but got up and with great effort managed to catch the leaders. With only 20 yards left in the race, he was in third place, good enough to qualify for the finals. He looked over his shoulder to the inside, and seeing no one, he slowed down. But another runner, charging hard on the outside, passed Coglan a yard before the finish line, eliminating him from the finals. Coglan's great comeback was rendered worthless because he slowed down and failed to run through the finish line.[7]

Don't quit before the finish line. Run through, not to, the finish line. This is easier said than done. Nehemiah has a moment in his life purpose race when he could have easily quit too soon. Outside forces beyond his control suddenly appear and threaten to derail the construction project. The threat comes from three specific sources: distractions, rumors and intimidation. Any one of these threats could paralyze progress on the wall. Only through the wise leadership skills of the cupbearer-turned-contractor named Nehemiah is the threat neutralized. The incident is described in detail in chapter six of Nehemiah's journal. Thankfully, Nehemiah does not quit too soon. From his example, we learn what it takes to finish strong in finding and fulfilling our life purpose.

Describe a time in your life when you quit too soon.

_____

_____

_____

_____

Don't Quit Because of Distractions (Nehemiah 6:1-4)

Nehemiah's enemies try to distract him by inviting him to a leader's conference at a place called Ono. *"Sanballat and Geshem sent me this message: 'Come, let us meet together in one of the villages on the plain of Ono'"* (v. 2). Nehemiah wisely says, "Oh, no!" to Ono because Ono is a no no! He refuses to be distracted from completing his life purpose. Instead, Nehemiah sends messengers to his enemies with a clear, concise and uncompromising RSVP to their invitation. Listen carefully to his response. *"I am carrying on a great project and cannot go down. Why should the work stop while I leave it and go down to you?"* (v. 3). His distracters do not want to take no for an answer. Four times they send Nehemiah the invitation and four times he says, "No!" Nehemiah is on a mission from God and nothing will be allowed to distract him from completing the task.

You can expect plenty of distractions along the way that will attempt to draw you away from finishing your life purpose. Some of these distractions may come from unexpected places. For example, you may encounter distractions from well-meaning family members who have a different agenda and vision for your life. Perhaps you have been on the receiving end of the old *God loves you and I have a wonderful plan for your life distraction*. Your life mission might seem strange and radical to them, so they will encourage you to take a safer path. Their hearts may be in the right place, but they don't have the mind of Christ for the journey God has mapped out for you. Get ready for this distraction because chances are high that it will come your way.

Materialism and the unhealthy pursuit of stuff can become a distraction for you, especially if God's blueprint for your life does not appear to be very lucrative. I have seen people walk away from God's call to full-time ministry because of financial reasons. They felt the pressure from family and friends to go into a more profitable field so they could make more money and keep up with the Jones'. Later they discovered the Jones family is not really happy. Someone has described keeping up with the Jones' as using money you don't have to buy things you don't need to impress people you don't like. Paul was correct when he warned Timothy, *"People who want to get rich fall into temptation and a trap and into many foolish and harmful desires that plunge men into ruin and destruction. For the love of money is the root of all kinds of evil. Some people, eager for money, have wandered from the faith and pierced themselves with many griefs"* (I Timothy 6:9-10). Imagine the painful grief of the people who get to the end of their lives and realize they made a lot of money, but they wandered away from God's plan.

Other distractions may come simply from living in a fallen world with ungodly morals and values. Lust and immorality have sabotaged many life missions. We have all seen more than our share of good people whose journeys began in the right direction, but were tragically shipwrecked by sinful choices. Hardly a year goes by that we don't see a news report of another pastor or ministry leader who has fallen into sin. The consequences are devastating to a leader's life mission and many never recover from the fall. Even when repentance happens and forgiveness is extended, the crippling consequences are never overcome. The leader's dash is irrevocably damaged.

You must also realize that not all distractions are evil in and of themselves. Even good things can become a distraction if they are allowed to interfere with God's best for your life. Good and noble projects can sap away your time and energy from what is best. Sometimes the greatest enemy of God's best is settling for something good, but less than God's ideal plan.

This leads us to a critical principle in successfully finding and fulfilling our life mission. Most people are wired by God in such a way that they can either do many things mediocrely or a few things really well. The person who is a jack of all trades but a master of none will tend to be distracted by many opportunities. A multitude of distractions has a way of spreading a person's time and energy too thin, greatly reducing one's effectiveness. Such a person will have a record of being an inch deep and a mile wide when it comes to impacting the world. Nehemiah's primary task of building the wall around Jerusalem could have been greatly delayed, or never even completed, if he had allowed the meeting of Ono to distract him.

Nehemiah teaches us an essential lesson in successfully living our dash: *learn to say no to any and all distractions which would lead you away from your God-inspired vision.* Don't let evil temptations or even good projects detour you from God's best. You have a choice: you can either be like a floodlight or a laser beam. A floodlight spreads its energy broadly, but lacks power. A laser beam concentrates its power and can cut through steel. You have to decide if you want to cut steel with your life mission.

Concentrating your focus and energy in this way can be a tremendous challenge if you find it difficult to say no to people, especially people you love and who love you. They may mean well, but they don't necessarily know God's best for your life. You must remember, like Nehemiah, that you are carrying on a great project. You must be ready when distractions come so that you do not get caught unprepared.

Successfully maneuvering your way through these kinds of distractions requires the development of two essential skills: wise discernment and the art of thinking fast. Notice Nehemiah does not require a long period of time to ponder and contemplate whether or not he should attend the Ono Conference. Such an investment of time is unnecessary because Nehemiah has developed the ability of making wise decisions and making them quickly. Have you developed the skills of discernment and the art of thinking fast?

Leadership author and speaker John Maxwell tells a humorous story that teaches the importance of these two essential skills. One day a hunting dog wandered off into the jungle and got lost. Suddenly, he noticed a leopard slowly stalking him, obviously wanting him for dinner. The dog had to think fast. Seeing a pile of bones nearby, the dog turned his back to the approaching leopard, laid down beside the pile of bones and started licking one of the them. Just as the leopard was ready to pounce on him, the dog said in a loud voice, "That sure was a delicious leopard!" The leopard quickly retreated and thought, "That was close. That sly dog almost had me!" Meanwhile, a monkey was watching the entire episode from the tree above. Wanting to gain future protection from the leopard, the monkey caught up to the leopard and told him about the dog's trick. The leopard was furious and turned to go back and eat the dog. When the dog saw the leopard and monkey coming back, he again had to think fast. Just as the leopard was about to pounce on him, the dog said in a loud voice, "Now where is that monkey? I sent him to get me another leopard 30 minutes ago!"

James 1:5 reminds us, *"If any of you lacks wisdom, he should ask God, who gives generously to all without finding fault, and it will be given to him."* As you seek to live out your life purpose, ask God daily for his guiding wisdom and quick discernment so that you can make good decisions when distractions try to lure you away from God's purpose for your life.

Tragically, we all know heartbreaking stories from individuals who did not practice wisdom in the face of distractions. Just think of the depressing story of Samson. Here was a man with outstanding promise and potential. Samson was chosen by God from birth with a powerful life mission. An angel of the Lord announced to Samson's mother before his birth that her son would be *"set apart to God from birth, and he will begin the deliverance of Israel from the hands of the Philistines"* (Judges 13:5). How's that for a God-size vision? Samson was destined to be one of God's powerful deliverers for the Israelites. He had the God-given opportunity to rid the Promised Land of the evil Philistines who had been a thorn in the side of Israel since the day Joshua led them into their homeland. Like Nehemiah, Samson had a great life mission from God and had the potential to accomplish great things for God. However, he squandered most of the opportunities during his life because he failed to handle distractions with wisdom and discernment. One name summarizes Samson's life of distractions: Delilah.

We remember the tragic end of Samson's life when the Philistines captured him and gouged out his eyes. But the more disastrous part of his story is that Samson lost his spiritual vision years earlier when he allowed ungodly distractions to cloud his vision of God's plan and purpose for his life. Distractions became for Samson like spiritual cataracts, blocking the clear vision of God's will for his life mission. The same can happen to us when we do not learn how to handle distractions with wisdom and discernment.

Jesus well understands the danger of distractions. One day two different men approach Jesus, both men wanting to be his disciples. However, both are turned down by Jesus because they are victims of distractions. Their stories are recorded in Luke 9:59-62. The first says, *"Lord, let me first go and bury my father."* The second says, *"I will follow you, Lord; but first let me go back and say goodbye to my family."* Notice the phrase repeated by both men: *"first let me."* Both men allowed their personal agendas to distract them from following Christ. This is why Jesus replies to these excuses, *"No one who puts his hand to the plow and looks back is fit for service in the kingdom of God."* This is the choice every would-be Christ follower will face. Will the decision be *Lord first* or will it be *first let me?*

We see the opposite response when we read the story of the calling of Elisha. The story begins when the Prophet Elijah is getting old and his ministry is beginning to wind down. It is time to hand the baton of leadership to a new prophet, a man named Elisha. Elisha is a farmer by trade and a rather well-off farmer. He owns and operates 12 yoke of oxen, a sign in that day and time of substantial wealth. He has considerable livestock, farm equipment and a number of employees. One day Elijah walks up to him and throws his cloak around him, a symbol of his passing on the mantle of leadership to Elisha. What Elisha does next is surprising and shocking. *"He took his yoke of oxen and slaughtered them. He burned the plowing equipment to cook the meat and gave it to the people, and they ate. Then he set out to follow Elijah and became his attendant"* (I Kings 19:21).

Elisha's unusual actions teach us two lasting principles of what it means to avoid distractions and follow God. First, Elisha shows us that following God wholeheartedly is a celebration, not a burden. Take a closer look at what he does. He throws a going-away barbeque with all the trimmings. Elisha does not approach this new calling with a long face or by creating a somber mood. He shows his family and friends that being a fully devoted follower of God is an honor to celebrate, not a decision to grieve. What a great reminder for us when we sign on the dotted line to do a great work for God. Ultimately, any sacrifice we make for God is no sacrifice at all. Following God should be more like a party, not a funeral. We should be guided by the now famous words of Jim Elliott, the missionary who gave his life trying to reach the Auca Indians of Ecuador – *"He is no fool who gives up what he cannot keep to gain that which he cannot lose."*

> Ultimately, any sacrifice we make for God is no sacrifice at all. Following God should be more like a party, not a funeral.

A second lesson Elisha's example teaches us is the importance of not looking back. In burning his plows and killing his oxen, Elisha is effectively eliminating any temptation to return to his old life. He removes the potential distractions from his life. There is no chance of Elisha changing his mind if following God doesn't work out. He is all in. There is no going back. I recall reading about the famous Spanish explorer Cortez who landed in Vera Cruz in 1519 to begin his conquest of Mexico with a small force of 700 men. Legend has it that Cortez intentionally set fire to his 11 ships to remove any means of retreat for his men. As his men stood on the beach and watched their ships burn, they realized there was no turning back.[8] Cortez had effectively removed a major distraction. Elisha does the same in burning his plows and killing his oxen.

Nehemiah's warning is clear: watch out for distractions. They can do great damage and cause major delays in completing your life mission. The message from Ono is a strong warning for anyone seeking to complete a great work for God; when your enemies want to distract you, don't take the bait. Instead, be prepared to think fast and make wise decisions. Like Nehemiah, learn to say, "No!" to your Ono. When distractions come, and they will, don't quit before the finish line.

What distractions consistently divert your attention from fulfilling your life purpose?

_____

_____

_____

_____

Don't Quit Because of Rumors (Nehemiah 6:5-9)

Have you ever been distracted and demoralized by rumors? There is nothing more discouraging and disheartening than being attacked by vicious rumors that distort the truth and discredit your reputation. As the construction of the wall nears completion, Sanballat tries to sidetrack Nehemiah by spreading false rumors. He accuses Nehemiah of leading the Jews in a revolt with the ultimate goal of declaring himself to be king. He even sends a letter to Nehemiah filled with the false accusations he and others are spreading. *"It is reported among the nations – and Geshem says it is true – that you and the Jews are plotting to revolt, and therefore you are building the wall. Moreover, according to these reports you are about to become their king and have appointed prophets to make this proclamation about you in Jerusalem: 'There is a king in Judah!'"* (6:6-7).

Sanballat concludes his letter to Nehemiah with a not-so-subtle threat that he will personally make sure King Artaxerxes gets this news: *"Now this report will get back to the king; so come, let us confer together"* (v.7). Sanballat's effort to spread rumors and blackmail Nehemiah is not the kind of distraction he needs, especially at this critical stage in the construction of the wall. The wall is nearing completion. Now is not the time for Nehemiah to have to put out rumor fires. Now is the time for single-minded concentration so he can finish the project.

Nehemiah wisely refuses to get caught up in Sanballat's scheme. We can learn from his two-fold response, which is brilliant and effective. First, he speaks the truth. The rumor is not true. *"Nothing like what you are saying is happening; you are just making it up out of your head"* (v. 8). Nehemiah does not waste valuable time mounting an elaborate defense. No letters to the editors are written. No press conferences are scheduled to correct the false rumors. Nehemiah is too smart to get sucked into this conflict. He recognizes the underlying motive of the attack is to demoralize his team, causing them to give up before the wall is completed. *"They were all trying to frighten us, thinking, 'Their hands will get too weak for the work, and it will not be completed'"* (v. 9). Nehemiah doesn't fall for the trick. He takes just enough time to set the record straight and avoids getting sucked into a time-consuming verbal battle with his enemies.

Second, he prays to God. What a simple, yet profound prayer he offers to God at the end of verse nine. *"Now strengthen my hands."* This is the kind of resolve it takes to finish strong when you find yourself on the wrong end of lies and rumors. God knows the truth and ultimately what he knows is all that matters. You must know in your heart that God is the ultimate source of strength to complete your life purpose. As Nehemiah will say later, *"The joy of the Lord is your strength"* (Nehemiah 8:10). The necessary strength to successfully handle rumors will not come from well-worded rebuttals, but from Almighty God's ability to strengthen your hands. Find your joy in his strength.

I had to personally learn this lesson the hard way. When I was a young pastor, I got wind of a rumor floating around town about me. The rumor was not true, so I decided to put an end to the gossip by tracking down its source. My goal was to find and confront the source of the rumor, set the record straight and then let the truth vindicate me. I was certain that the truth would then spread around town as quickly as the rumor. I began early one morning and spent the better part of the day chasing the rumor. All day I drove around town from house to house and office to office in search of the original source of the rumor. By the end of the day, I still could not nail down the source. It seemed like the people closest to the rumor had a sudden case of amnesia. They could not recall where they first heard the rumor. The only fact they were all certain of was that they were not the original source of the rumor.

I learned a valuable lesson from my day-long, rumor-chasing experience: *If you try to track down a rumor, all you will find at the end of the day is that you have wasted a day!* You will have better luck nailing Jello to a tree than nailing down the source of a rumor. I would have been wiser to follow Nehemiah's example and spend the day in prayer. I would have saved a wasted day and a tank of gasoline.

Being a target of vicious rumors comes with being a leader, so don't feel alone when you are the victim. You are actually in very good company. Walk through the pages of the Bible and you will see how often its great heroes were the victims of rumors. Imagine the kinds of rumors Noah must have endured while he built the Ark. Recall the false reports spread by the rebellious Israelites about Moses during the 40 years in the wilderness. Remember how the Old Testament prophets were ridiculed and falsely accused of being in league with the enemies of Israel.

Even Jesus himself was the victim of numerous rumors. At one point in his public ministry, his critics spread the false report that he was casting out demons by the power of Satan. As crazy as it sounds, rumors even floated around Jerusalem that Jesus was a *"glutton and drunkard"* (Matthew 11:19). Jesus never wasted his time trying to chase down the source of his rumors. He had no doubt about the ultimate source of all lies being none other than Satan himself. *"When he lies, he speaks his native language, for he is a liar and the father of lies"* (John 8:44). Jesus responded to rumors and false accusations very much like Nehemiah. When confronted with a rumor, he clarified the truth for those willing to listen and then moved on with his ministry. He refused to be distracted by rumors. We must come to grips with the fact that rumors come with the leadership territory. We must, however, remember another great truth from the examples of these great leaders. They all refused to let rumors detour them from accomplishing God's plan for their lives.

Don't let rumors sidetrack you from pursuing your life purpose. There is a choice to be made when it comes to dealing with rumors. You can either spend your time chasing down rumors or you can spend your time chasing down your God-given mission in life. You do not have time to do both. When rumors come, and they will, don't quit before the finish line.

Describe a time when you have been distracted and demoralized by rumors?

_____

_____

_____

_____

How do you typically respond to false rumors about yourself? What changes do you need to make?

_____

_____

_____

_____

_____

Don't Quit Because of Intimidation (Nehemiah 6:10-19)

When distractions and rumors fail to stop Nehemiah and the construction project, his enemies try a third tactic: intimidation. If you have ever been intimidated by a bully, you know how the experience can leave you feeling weak and helpless. Nehemiah's enemies try to intimidate him in two ways. First, they use intimidating prophets. Tobiah and Sanballat hire false prophets for one purpose: to intimidate Nehemiah. They basically tell Nehemiah there is a contract out on his life, so he better hide in the temple for protection. However, Nehemiah refuses to be intimidated. *"Should a man like me run away? Or should one like me go into the temple to save his life? I will not go!"* (v.11). He sees through the scheme and understands the hidden motive of these false prophets is to *"intimidate me so that I would commit a sin by doing this, and then they would give me a bad name to discredit me"* (v. 13).

Second, they use intimidating letters. Nehemiah's enemies begin a letter-writing campaign hoping to discredit and distract him. Again, Nehemiah recognizes the motive behind the false letters. *"Tobiah sent letters to intimidate me"* (v. 19). But Nehemiah refuses to be intimidated by these tactics. He resists the temptation to be paralyzed by fear. Instead, he once again turns his critics over to God in prayer. *"Remember Tobiah and Sanballat, O my God, because of what they have done; remember also the prophetess Noadiah and the rest of the prophets who have been trying to intimidate me"* (v. 14).

Successful leaders must master the ability to handle intimidation. Otherwise, they will be paralyzed by it. History is filled with examples of people who refused to be controlled by intimidating people or circumstances. Can you identify this man? He failed in business in '31. He was defeated for the legislature in '32, but elected in '34. His sweetheart died in '35. He had a nervous breakdown in '36. He was defeated for speaker in '38 and defeated for elector in '40. He was defeated for Congress in '43, elected in '46, but defeated again in '48. He was defeated for the Senate in '50, defeated for Vice President in '56 and defeated for the Senate in '58. But fortunately he did not quit before the finish line. Abraham Lincoln was elected President of the United States in 1860. He refused to be intimidated by defeat.[9]

Wilma Rudolph refused to be intimidated by her physical handicaps. She suffered from polio as a child, leaving her with a crooked leg. She wore metal braces for over six years. At age 11, Wilma forced herself to walk without braces. At age 12, she started running. By the time Wilma reached high school, she was outrunning every other girl on the team. In 1956, she ran in the Melbourne Olympics, winning the bronze medal. At the Rome Olympics in 1960, she won three gold medals. Wilma Rudolph did not quit before the finish line.

In his book *Pursuit of Excellence*, Ted Engstrom observes, "Cripple him and you have a Sir Walter Scott. Lock him in a prison cell, and you have a John Bunyan. Bury him in the snows of Valley Forge, and you have a George Washington. Strike him with infantile paralysis and he becomes a Franklin Roosevelt. Deafen him, and you have a Ludwig van Beethoven. Have him born black in a society filled with racial discrimination, and you have a Booker T. Washington or a George Washington Carver. Call him a slow learner, 'retarded,' and write him off as uneducable, and you have an Albert Einstein."[10] All of these people were determined to overcome and defeat the intimidating critics and circumstances.

Like these individuals, Nehemiah refuses to give up and give in to intimidation. Does it pay off? Absolutely. The wall is completed and the enemies are depleted. *"So the wall was completed on the twenty-fifth of Elul, in fifty-two days. When our enemies heard about this, all the surrounding nations were afraid and lost their self-confidence, because they realized that this work had been done with the help of our God"* (vv. 15-16).

The wall is completed because Nehemiah refuses to be sidetracked by the intimidating tactics of his enemies. They are relentless in their attacks, but Nehemiah outlasts them all. He wins the day with perseverance. He refuses to quit. The same will be true for you. When intimidation comes, and it will, don't quit before the finish line.

> What are the sources of intimidation in your life that keep you from fulfilling your life purpose?
>
> _____
>
> _____
>
> _____
>
> _____

In today's culture of entitlements and instant everything, I fear we may be losing our grip on the virtue of perseverance. It's understandable because perseverance involves the undesirable experiences of pain, hard work and delayed gratification. We don't like to work for and wait for something to happen because we have grown accustomed to immediate satisfaction. I fear we may be losing the pleasure that comes only when we persevere to the end and reach the goal. A diminishing number of people know the sweet joy of running the race hard and winning the victory hidden just on the other side of the finish line.

When I think of the importance of perseverance and not quitting too soon, I think of the story of politician Mario Cuomo when he ran for governor of New York in 1982. At one point in the campaign, he was tired, depressed and ready to quit. But he remembered an incident from his childhood. Their family had just moved into a house which had a 40-foot blue spruce in the yard. One day a terrible storm hit the area and almost pulled the blue spruce totally out of the ground. The top of the tree was lying on the asphalt of the street in front of the house. Mario remembered how his heart sank when he saw the uprooted tree. But his five-foot, six-inch Italian Pappa said, "OK, we gonna push 'im up!" The rest of the family said, "But Pappa, the roots are out of the ground." But Pappa refused to be deterred and said, "Shut up...we gonna push 'im up; he's gonna grow again!"

So they got ropes, tied them to the tree, and in the rain they pulled up the great blue spruce. Pappa dug in the mud until the tree roots sank lower and lower. The rest of the family shoveled mud over the roots. Then they moved boulders to the base of the tree to keep it in place and tied the ropes from tree limbs to stakes in the ground. After hours of work, Pappa said, "Don't worry; he's gonna grow again."

As Mario Cuomo remembered this childhood event, he smiled because he knew that if he drove past their old home, he would see that great blue spruce standing tall, now 65-feet high. Inspired by this memory, Mario did not drop out of the race. He persevered and went on to win the 1982 election because he refused to quit before the finish line.

One of the great themes found throughout the Bible is the power of perseverance. As believers, we are repeatedly challenged to never give up. We especially hear this exhortation in the Book of Hebrews. This New Testament letter was first written to a group of Christ followers who must have been terribly discouraged. They were experiencing opposition and the early stages of persecution for their Christian faith. Some who were Jewish Christians were especially disheartened. They were actually abandoning their faith in Christ and were returning to Judaism to avoid persecution. They were ready to throw in the towel. So the writer of Hebrews takes pen in hand and sets out to encourage these discouraged saints to finish strong and not give up before the finish line.

On practically every page of Hebrews the writer seems to be shouting, "Don't quit before you reach the finish line!" This message of finishing strong reaches a crescendo in chapter 12 when the writer paints a word picture of a runner in a race. Listen to his don't-give-up message. *"Therefore, since we are surrounded by such a great cloud of witnesses, let us throw off everything that hinders and the sin that so easily entangles, and let us run with perseverance the race marked out for us"* (Hebrews 12:1).

Notice the word perseverance in this verse. The Greek word used here is *hypomone*. This is a compound word in the Greek, meaning to abide under; to bear up under. It is a picture of a donkey bearing up under a heavy load. Does this describe how you feel at this point in your race toward fulfilling your life mission? Nehemiah would be the first to tell you that the load can be heavy at times, especially when you are feeling the pressures of distractions, rumors and intimidations. But Nehemiah would also be the first to encourage you to persevere to the finish line.

Could you use one additional role model to lead the way? The writer of Hebrews provides the perfect mentor for us to follow. Following his challenge to run the race with perseverance, he provides this example for us to follow. *"Let us fix our eyes on Jesus, the author and perfecter of our faith, who for the joy set before him endured the cross, scorning its shame, and sat down at the right hand of God. Consider him who endured such opposition from sinful men, so that you will not grow weary and lose heart"* (Hebrews 12:2-3).

Run hard. Don't stop now. Don't grow weary and lose heart. The finish line is closer today than it has ever been before.

In what ways are you being tempted right now to quit before the finish line?

_____

_____

_____

_____

_____

Living My Dash: Don't Quit Before the Finish Line

Ask the average pastor how often he is tempted to quit the ministry and, if he is honest, he will answer, "Once a week... every Monday morning!" After a long, exhausting weekend, some pastors crawl out of bed on Monday morning and don't even believe in God until noon. This is why Monday is generally not a pastor's best day for making major decisions and certainly not the best day for counseling people in crisis. Combine fatigue with a loss of adrenaline and many pastors begin their week singing, *Rainy days and Mondays always get me down.* Most pastors learn rather quickly that feeling tired and weary on Mondays is par for the course and not a major concern. But what happens when Mondays start bleeding over into Tuesdays and Wednesdays? What happens when discouragement sets in and doesn't go away?

Sustaining my life purpose was not easy in the early days of the new church plant. Even though I loved what I was doing, I still had my moments when selling life insurance certainly looked attractive. I could identify with Nehemiah's three derailers of distractions, rumors and intimidation. I felt like I was becoming a close friend of all three. Any one of the three was enough to make me want to cash in my chips and call it a life.

In the early days, I had my share of distractions. Some family members and friends thought I was making a big mistake starting a new church at my age and they were not afraid to tell me so. Others told me I should move and find an established church in another city to pastor. At one point, I was even offered a rather lucrative business opportunity, which would have meant leaving full-time pastoral ministry. I will never forget the experience. The business man making me the offer handed me a set of car keys and said, "Rick, there's a Cadillac parked outside in your driveway. It's yours if you take the job."

It was tough for me to say, "No at Ono!" Remember, I had a wife, two teenagers and a mortgage. Plus, I thought I would look pretty good driving around town in that Cadillac. There were plenty of days when the thought of starting over with a new church plant was overwhelming and intimidating. Having already planted one church, I knew the work ahead of me. How could I lead this new church of over 400 members without additional staff and where would I find future staff members willing to come to a small town to a church without a building? Was I up for the challenge, or would it be wiser to rent a U-Haul truck and take an easier path?

Add to the mix another challenge: the rumor mill of a small town. Leaving one church and starting a new church in the same small town is a breeding ground for rumors. I couldn't believe some of the stories being told around town of things I had said, deeds I had done, deals I had cut, secret meetings I had organized. I learned about clandestine meetings I had led even though I had not even been present at the meetings. I also learned about other meetings where I was the topic of discussion, but not an invited guest.

Rumors started to take wings and fly around town. I remembered from past experience the futility of trying to track down rumors, so I resisted the temptation. But there were difficult and discouraging days when the rumors felt like the intimidating giants faced by the twelve spies sent by Moses to check out the Promised Land. Let me tell you, that grasshopper-complex-syndrome is real. I felt small and I felt like quitting. But by the grace of God, I did not quit. As Nehemiah would say, *"God strengthened my hands"* and I have lived to experience the joy found at the finish line of perseverance.

Perseverance… hypomone. The message is the same regardless of the language. Don't give up and don't give in to the pressure to quit before the finish line. I have decided to follow for the rest of my life the advice of author H. Jackson Brown in his book, *Life's Little Instruction Book*, where he offers the following prescription for those days when you feel like quitting:

- Rule #1: Take one more step.
- Rule #2: When you can't take one more step, refer back to Rule #1.[11]

75

Looking in the rearview mirror, I am glad I did not quit before the finish line. Overcoming distractions, rumors and intimidations has not always been easy, and even today facing these enemies is not my favorite part of living my dash. But I must honestly say the rewards have already been eternal. I know I am serving in my sweet spot and daily fulfilling God's purpose for my life. I now see how God was using those hard times to make me strong, preparing me not only to fulfill my life purpose, but also to equip me to encourage others facing similar challenges.

What is your life purpose? What is the one task God wants you to accomplish in your life between now and your funeral? Has it been put on the shelf because of distractions, rumors or intimidation? Then it is time for you to pull it off the shelf, dust it off and get it started again. Learn from the example of Nehemiah. Don't quit before the finish line. I'm glad I refused to quit and I know you will be glad, too. Don't quit and you will be well on your way to successfully living your dash.

CHAPTER 5 – DON'T QUIT BEFORE THE FINISH LINE

Living Your Dash

Step #1: Don't Quit Because of Distractions (Nehemiah 6:1-4)
I understand that when I become focused on fulfilling God's purpose for my life, others will seek to distract me and tempt me to quit. Rather than abandoning my calling, I will think fast, be ready, and wisely learn to stay focused on the goal God has given me.

Step #2: Don't Quit Because of Rumors (Nehemiah 6:5-9)
I will not succumb to the rumors used by those who tempt me to quit. Rather than give in to rumors, I will speak the truth and place my trust in God to defend me from false accusation.

Step #3: Don't Quit Because of Intimidation (Nehemiah 6:10-19)
Rather than allowing others to intimidate me, I will keep my focus upon God's calling and provision. I will honestly assess both my strengths and weaknesses, and allow God to use both in guiding me to fulfill my life purpose.

Father God,

Way too often, I am tempted to put my life purpose on the shelf because of distractions, rumors or intimidation. I allow my focus to shift away from you to my distracters or weaknesses. Give me the confidence of Nehemiah to stand up to my distractions, address the rumors, and refuse to be intimidated by anyone again. Give me the strength to never quit before the finish line, but rather to finish life hearing you say, "Well done, my good and faithful servant!"

In Jesus name I pray, Amen.

PART II

FULFILLING YOUR LIFE PURPOSE

THE LANDING

So you think takeoffs can be tense times. Just hang around for the landings, as if you have a choice! Some of my most frightening moments in life have involved the final descents. One of the greatest understatements on the planet is spoken by pilots: "Ladies and gentlemen, we may experience some turbulence in our final descent." The layman's interpretation: "You are about to get closer to God than you have ever been before in your entire lifetime. I hope your will is in order in case we don't make it. The next few moments are guaranteed to make even a Protestant cross himself!"

Landing your life purpose can be a challenging experience because it involves developing a plan for the long haul. Once you have your life purpose up and running, you must plan for the future. Important questions must be asked and difficult issues must be addressed. What kind of maintenance issues will I encounter? How can I sustain quality over the long haul? What kind of internal and external controls must be in place to maintain integrity and accountability? What will it take to finish strong so that I can leave a lasting legacy?

I have had my share of turbulent landings over the years, especially during thunderstorms. But I always find myself repeating the same action while descending through the wind and rain. I look out the window until I can see the runway lights. When I see those two lines of lights out front, my confidence grows and my anxiety subsides. I know the pilot now has a visual target out his windshield. All he has to do now is stay between the lines.

In the second half of his journal, Nehemiah demonstrates how to successfully maintain your life mission over time, even during the most turbulent conditions. He also teaches you how to stay between the lines at critical times so that you can successfully complete your journey and safely land your life mission. This effective leader will provide you with a number of significant guiding principles which are designed to be like runway lights to steer you safely to your final destination.

That's not to suggest that flying and landing your life purpose will be easy. Nehemiah's experience will make that crystal clear. In fact, you better buckle up for this next section of our study because the flight is about to get rough. But follow Nehemiah's advice through your entire life mission flight, and at the end, you should be able to shout, "Touchdown!"

As we move from Part 1: *Finding your Life Purpose* to Part 2: *Fulfilling your Life Purpose*, summarize your God-given Life Purpose as best you can at this point in your journey.

_____

_____

_____

_____

_____

_____

_____

_____

_____

_____

_____

_____

_____

_____

_____

_____

_____

_____

_____

_____

Now, summarize your Life Purpose into two words.

_____   _____

CHAPTER SIX

MAINTAIN YOUR VISION

It's what you learn after you know it all that counts.
John Wooden

In three words I can summarize everything I've learned about life: it goes on.
Robert Frost

In my years as a pastor of several local churches, I have been involved in a total of seven church building projects. Some have been smaller to medium size remodel/ renovation type projects; others have been full-scale, multi-million dollar building programs. Regardless of the size and scope of these projects, I have noticed a common denominator in every one of them. Every construction project has had two distinct phases: the construction phase and the maintenance phase. In fact, the budgets for these building projects were divided into a construction budget and a maintenance budget. Even the bank loan was divided into two distinct parts: the construction loan and the permanent loan.

The same is true with living your dash. You can expect to experience a *finding phase* and a *fulfilling phase* in your life purpose journey. The first phase will tend to focus on constructing your purpose. During this phase, you will focus your time and energy on specific goals like catching and clarifying God's vision, getting confirmation and buy-in from the significant people in your life, and overcoming various obstacles in getting your vision off the ground. The second phase will be very different, requiring an entirely different set of skills. The primary focus of your time and energy during this phase will be on learning and developing the leadership skills necessary to maintain your life purpose for the long haul.

For Nehemiah and his team, the wall is completed in a record-breaking 52 days. Some might conclude that once the wall is built, then Nehemiah's life purpose is complete. All that's left to do now is plan his retirement party and present Nehemiah with his gold watch. Nothing is further from the truth. The construction phase of his mission may be finished, but the maintenance phase is just beginning. There is a *spiritual upkeep* stage that is essential to the long-term success of his life purpose.

You will find the same is true with living your dash. Maintaining the focus and direction of your mission is a life-long commitment with new challenges around every corner. Like driving a car, you may be on the road traveling in the right direction, but you cannot let go of the wheel. There are constant corrections and adjustments that must be made or you will land your life mission in the ditch. Keeping your mission on the road will require on-going maintenance and diligent attention.

The second half of Nehemiah's journal describes the events surrounding the maintenance phase of the project. Chapters 8 through 13 teach you how to maintain your life purpose in such a way as to maximize long term success. In these chapters, Nehemiah focuses on four key areas which require his careful attention: vision, values, gratitude and integrity. Success will demand that you also give diligent attention to these same four areas.

Nehemiah begins with a challenge to maintain the vision of your life purpose. You quickly discover as a leader that vision leaks. Just because your vision bucket was full during the initial phase of your project does not guarantee that it will remain full long-term. Your team may start out with a solid understanding of the vision. However, as time passes so does the vision. What was once crystal clear becomes cloudy and out of focus. It takes a wise leader to re-envision the troops.

What will it take for you and your team to catch and maintain a renewed vision of your life mission? What will keep you traveling on the right road and out of the ditch? Ask Nehemiah and he will answer unapologetically, the word of God. Like a compass in a storm, God's word can keep you focused and on track in fulfilling your life purpose. For Nehemiah, the application of specific scriptures is amazingly relevant to his situation and proves to be extremely helpful in keeping the vision clearly before the people. You will discover a similar relevance as you dig into the word of God. You might even get the impression at times that God wrote certain passages in the Bible with your life mission in mind.

> The Bible describes itself as a light that illuminates our path (Psalm 119:105). How are you allowing God's word to guide you toward fulfilling your life purpose?
>
> _____
>
> _____
>
> _____
>
> _____

Read God's Word with Reverence (Nehemiah 8:1-8)

When we hear the word Watergate, it reminds us of a time of spiritual vacuum in our nation. But for Nehemiah, the word reminds him of a time of great spiritual renewal. The physical construction of the wall around Jerusalem is now finished. Now it is time for a spiritual rebuilding of the People of God and it happens at a place called the Water Gate. This is the location in Jerusalem where the people of Israel gather to read the word of God and we discover they read it with great reverence. *"All the people assembled as one man in the square before the Water Gate. They told Ezra the scribe to bring out the Book of the Law of Moses, which the Lord had commanded for Israel. So on the first day of the seventh month Ezra the priest brought the law before the assembly, which was made up of men and women and all who were able to understand"* (vv. 1-2).

Nehemiah, Ezra and the other leaders realize the importance of firmly planting the word of God as the future guide for the People of God. Israel would need to see the Scripture as their ultimate and authoritative guidebook in order for them to experience God's ongoing blessing, favor and protection. The wall around the city could protect them from invading armies. But knowing and obeying the truth of God's word could protect them from the attack of sinful influences, or as the Apostle Paul would later say, *"Against the powers of this dark world and against the spiritual forces of evil in the heavenly realms"* (Ephesians 6:12).

The same is true for us today. We desperately need a renewed commitment and radical devotion to the word of God as our authoritative guide for living. One of the greatest problems facing the church today is Biblical illiteracy. Many Christians own multiple copies of the Bible, but fail to read and study God's word. Several years ago, a test of Bible knowledge was given to five classes of high school seniors. Most of them failed the exam completely. Some were so confused they thought Sodom and Gomorrah were lovers, and the four Gospels were written by Matthew, Mark, Luther and John. Others thought Eve was created from an apple and the stories Jesus used in his teachings were called parodies. A Gallup poll revealed that 60 percent of Americans did not know what the Holy Trinity was, 66 percent could not say who delivered the Sermon on the Mount and 79 percent were unable to name a single Old Testament prophet. Tragically, the numbers are not much better for Americans who attend church.

How can you overcome Biblical illiteracy so that you can keep the vision of your life purpose in focus, on track and in line with the will of God? Israel's experience at the Water Gate can be instructive. Listen carefully to their four-fold response to Ezra as he reads from the Law of God.

First, you need to read God's word with attentiveness. Picture Ezra standing on a high wooden platform constructed for this special occasion. He opens the Law of God and begins to read. How will the people respond? *"He read it aloud from daybreak till noon as he faced the square before the Water Gate in the presence of the men, women and others who could understand. And all the people listened attentively to the Book of the Law"* (v. 3). There is always the temptation to listen to a sermon and say to yourself, "I sure wish so and so was here today. He sure needed to hear this message!" Or "I'm buying the CD of today's message for my spouse!" Our response to hearing God's word should instead be, "God, what are you saying to me?" This kind of attentiveness will keep your life purpose in line with God's will.

We are reminded of this same truth in James 1:22-25. *"Do not merely listen to the word, and so deceive yourselves. Do what it says. Anyone who listens to the word but does not do what it says is like a man who looks at his face in a mirror and, after looking at himself, goes away and immediately forgets what he looks like. But the man who looks intently into the perfect law that gives freedom, and continues to do this, not forgetting what he has heard, but doing it – he will be blessed in what he does."*

The compass and map for many modern travelers have been replaced in recent years with a device called a GPS, a global positioning system. Simply program in your desired destination and the GPS will display a map on the screen and even provide verbal commands to help you reach your destination. However, if you make a wrong turn at any point in the journey, a voice will make you aware of your mistake and will give new instructions to get you back on track. You will be gently rebuked by the voice saying, "recalculating" until you make the required adjustments. The word of God is designed to provide people with the same detailed instructions for daily living. The person wise enough to follow the commands will be, according to James, *"blessed in what he does."* In order for you to stay on course with your life purpose, you must be attentive to the word of God.

Second, you need to read God's word with awe. Nehemiah's journal continues to describe the response of the people on this special day. *"Ezra opened the book. All the people could see him because he was standing above them; and as he opened it, the people all stood up. Ezra praised the Lord, the great God; and all the people lifted their hands and responded, 'Amen! Amen!' Then they bowed down and worshiped the Lord with their faces to the ground"* (v. 5-6). What a powerful description of how to read God's word with awe.

My grandfather was a carpenter by trade. In his old, rusty tool box he kept a steel plumb line. It was roughly the size of a small egg and was shaped like an upside-down tear drop. With the point facing down and a cord attached to the other end, the plumb line was used to make sure a wall was "plumb" or straight. The cord was attached to the top of the wall and the plumb line was allowed to hang down. My grandfather would then align the wall to the plumb line before he nailed it in place.

The Old Testament prophet Amos used the plumb line as an analogy for God's law.

Amos rebuked Israel because they had not aligned their lives with the plumb line of God's word. *"The Lord was standing by a wall that had been built true to plumb, with a plumb line in his hand. And the Lord asked me, 'What do you see, Amos?' 'A plumb line,' I replied. Then the Lord said, 'Look, I am setting a plumb line among my people Israel; I will spare them no longer'"* (Amos 7:7-8).

God's word is not just another opinion or a divine suggestion to be considered among many options. It is the authoritative, inspired, final, the-buck-stops-here, word of God. When God drops the plumb line of his word, we must align our lives to its direction. Tragically, many Christians yield to the temptation of bending the word of God to fit their crooked lifestyle. Such a mistake can derail a person's life purpose. It is just a matter of time before a crooked wall falls down. Reading the word of God with awe will help keep your life purpose on course.

Third, you need to read God's word with accuracy. The primary goal of any good Bible teacher will always be to accurately teach the Scripture in its historical context, always seeking to find the author's original intention, so that the truth can be accurately applied to the lives of people. Ezra and his fellow teachers do their best to teach God's word with this kind of accuracy and precision. *"The Levites... instructed the people in the Law while the people were standing there. They read from the Book of the Law, making it clear and giving the meaning so that the people could understand what was being read"* (vv. 7-8). This is a powerful description of the kind of Bible teachers we still need today. We need men and women who will teach the Bible in such a way that they make it clear and give the meaning so that people can understand what is being read.

We see a similar admonition given by the Apostle Paul to his friend and fellow pastor, Timothy. *"Do your best to present yourself to God as one approved, a workman who does not need to be ashamed and who correctly handles the word of truth"* (I Timothy 2:15). The King James Version translates *"correctly handles the word of truth"* with the phrase *"rightly dividing the word of truth."* This translation helps paint the picture of a teacher correctly organizing the truth into the proper categories so that verses are not taken out of context and misapplied. Bad things happen when the word of God is *wrongly divided* and misapplied. Ezra and his team of teachers make certain that their teaching is rightly divided so that it is accurately interpreted and applied. This is a critical commitment you must make if you hope to reach your destination. It is impossible to maintain the vision of your life purpose if you mishandle the compass of God's word.

Fourth, read God's word with application. Reread the last phrase in verse eight and you will discover the ultimate goal of correctly handling Scripture: *"so that the people could understand what was being read."* Here is the second goal of a good Bible teacher: to help people understand how to correctly apply God's truth to their lives. The goal in teaching the Bible is never to be impressive, super-intellectual or cerebral. The teacher's target is always to make the Bible clear, giving its correct meaning so people will be able to understand and apply the truth of God's word to their lives. Nehemiah and his teaching team of Levites successfully achieve this goal.

Several years ago, a member of my church told me he and his wife decided to move their membership to another church. The reason he gave for the decision was that they were not being fed by my teaching, which he described as "shallow and superficial." It was my pleasure to recommend another church to the couple. But I understood what they were searching for. They had previously attended a church where the preaching was super-intellectual and cerebral, filled with Hebrew and Greek word studies and seminary level lectures every Sunday. I have known plenty of teachers like this who appealed only to those who could comprehend their lofty, intellectual dissertations.

Nehemiah 8:8 is one of my life verses as a Bible teacher. My goal when I stand before any group of people is always the same: make it clear and give the meaning so that people can understand and apply the message to their daily lives. Keeping the message simple and applicable has always been this teacher's target. I have come to understand that simple is neither shallow nor superficial. In fact, simple can actually be quite profound. Take Jesus' teaching for example. Jesus is the greatest teacher of all time, yet his teaching is simple and applicable. This is one reason why the common people loved his teachings so much. But I don't think anyone in their right mind would describe Jesus' teaching as shallow and superficial.

> My guiding rule is simple: if you cannot apply on Monday what I teach you on Sunday, then I just wasted our Sunday.

We see an illustration of this truth every time we read or recite the Lord's Prayer recorded in Matthew 6:9-13. In this section of the Sermon on the Mount, Jesus is teaching his disciples how to pray. So, technically this is an example of Jesus' teaching methodology. The New International Version translation of this famous prayer has a total of 52 words, of which 37 are monosyllable words. This means 71 percent of the words in the Lord's Prayer are single-syllable words. This is Jesus keeping it simple.

I challenge you to always *keep the cookies on the lower shelves* when you are teaching the Bible so more can enjoy a taste. I like using the KISS Method of teaching: Keep It Simple Saints. My guiding rule is simple: if you cannot apply on Monday what I teach you on Sunday, then I just wasted our Sunday.

This is what it takes for you to read the word of God with reverence. Keep these four words in mind when you read the word of God: attentiveness, awe, accuracy and application. Do this and the word of God will help you keep your life purpose on track.

> Ezra and the Levites instructed the people in the Law "so that the people could understand what was being read" (Neh. 8:7-8). Who do you consult to help you understand God's word?
>
> _____
>
> _____
>
> _____
>
> _____
>
> Describe a recent experience where God's word helped you stay on the path to fulfilling your Life Purpose?
>
> _____
>
> _____
>
> _____
>
> _____

Read God's Word with Rejoicing (Nehemiah 8:9-12)

As Ezra and his fellow teachers read and explain God's word, the people are deeply convicted of their sinfulness and are literally moved to tears. *"For all the people had been weeping as they listened to the words of the Law"* (v. 9). This response to the reading of God's word should come as no surprise. One of the legitimate purposes of scripture is to expose and correct sinful behavior. However, the goal is not to leave sinners wallowing in their guilt. The ultimate goal of guilt is to lead people to repentance and to the joy of God's forgiveness.

Nehemiah has to act decisively in order to move the people from a place of guilt to a place of grace. What he does next is a bit shocking and surprising. He declares a party. You heard that correctly. He declares a party so the people will stop mourning and start experiencing the joy of reading God's word. *"Nehemiah said, 'Go and enjoy choice food and sweet drinks, and send some to those who have nothing prepared. This day is sacred to our Lord.*

Do not grieve, for the joy of the Lord is our strength'" (v. 10).

Nehemiah is teaching what the Apostle Paul would later teach the Corinthian Church. Paul wrote these believers in order to confront them with a number of serious issues that needed to be corrected. They repented and made the needed corrections. However, this letter was blunt and caused them a great deal of sorrow. It seemed they were having trouble moving from guilt to grace, so Paul followed this harsh letter with a letter of affirmation, commending them for their repentance. In II Corinthians, he writes, *"Godly sorrow brings repentance that leads to salvation and leaves no regrets, but worldly sorrow brings death"* (II Corinthians 7:10). God's word is designed to bring people to conviction and a godly sorrow, but not leave them there. God wants to move people to a place of forgiveness, salvation and joy that leaves no regrets.

How will you respond when God's word exposes unhealthy and ungodly behavior in your life? Will you have the courage to face the truth, make the necessary changes and move forward in God's grace? The story is told that many years ago, while on a visit to England, a wealthy businessman was shown a powerful microscope. He decided to purchase the microscope and take it back home. He thoroughly enjoyed his new instrument until one day he examined some food he was preparing to eat for dinner. Much to his dismay, he discovered tiny, microscopic creatures crawling in it. Since he was especially fond of this particular food, he wondered what he should do. Finally, he concluded there was only one way out of the dilemma. He would have to destroy the microscope. So, he smashed it to pieces.[12] We hear this story and say, "How foolish!" But do we make the same mistake when the word of God exposes sin in our lives? Rather than change our behavior, we avoid the exposing word of God.

Let God's word keep the vision of your life purpose clear and focused. When you read the Scripture, let it convict you of sin and expose what needs to change. But then rejoice because God has shown you the truth and extends his forgiveness. Read God's word with rejoicing.

Describe a time in your past when you experienced the joy of being forgiven by God through confession and repentance.

_____

_____

_____

_____

What is God's word calling you to surrender to Him today in order to continue fulfilling your Life Purpose?

_____

_____

_____

_____

Read God's Word with Repetition (Nehemiah 8:13-18)

Nehemiah and the Israelites read God's word on the first day from daybreak until noon. They are back to read more from the Book of the Law on the second day. There is even a hint that they are beginning to develop a consistent habit of study. *"Day after day, from the first day to the last, Ezra read from the Book of the Law of God"* (v. 18). The more they read, the more they realize and understand the practical relevance the scripture has for their lives.

Something happens on the second day of reading that demonstrates just how practical and applicable the Book of the Law is becoming in their lives. At some point during the second day, Ezra is reading from the Law. He comes across a passage which addresses the detailed instructions concerning the observation of the Feast of Tabernacles or Booths. *"They found written in the Law, which the Lord had commanded through Moses, that the Israelites were to live in booths during the feast of the seventh month and that they should proclaim this word and spread it throughout their towns and in Jerusalem: 'Go out into the hill country and bring back branches from the olive and wild olive trees, and from myrtles, palms and shade trees, to make booths' – as it is written"* (vv. 14-15).

That's all it takes for the Israelites. The practice of daily reading God's word moves the people to obedience. *"So the people went out and brought back branches and built for themselves booths on their own roofs, in their courtyards, in the courts of the house of God and in the square by the Water Gate and the one by the Gate of Ephraim"* (v. 16). This is what happens when God's people develop the discipline of reading God's word. Here is an oversight on the part of Israel. They have not been observing the Feast of Tabernacles because they were ignorant of God's command. Once their ignorance is replaced with knowledge, the people are more than willing to obey the command and reinstitute the ordinance.

Have you made the study of God's word a consistent habit in your life? The Scripture must become the ongoing, guiding compass in fulfilling your life purpose. The truth of

God's word will help you maintain the true north of your vision. Nothing will change your life and guide your daily decisions like the regular, consistent, disciplined study of the scripture. God is willing and able to communicate with you. He has an amazing way of speaking in very practical and specific ways to guide and correct, but you will not hear his instructions if you are not immersed in the study of the Bible.

Years ago, I heard the true story of a man in Kansas City who was severely injured in an explosion. His face was badly disfigured and he lost his eyesight, as well as both hands. He was a new Christian and one of his greatest regrets was that he could no longer read the Bible. He heard about a lady in England who read braille with her lips. He gave it a try, but was disappointed when he discovered the nerve endings in his lips had been destroyed in the explosion. One day something surprising happened while he was experimenting with reading his braille Bible with his lips. As he brought one of the braille pages to his lips, his tongue accidently touched a few of the raised characters and he suddenly realized he could feel them. Like a flash he thought, "I can read the Bible with my tongue!" When I first read this man's story, he had already read the entire Bible from cover to cover four times with his tongue. What are your excuses for not habitually reading the Bible? When I read this man's story, my excuses dissolve.

How about you? Have you discovered the reward of consistently reading and then applying God's word to your life? King David was correct when he wrote these words concerning the commands of God. *"They are more precious than gold, than much pure gold; they are sweeter than honey, than honey from the honey comb. By them your servant is warned; in keeping them there is great reward"* (Psalm 19:10-11). Read God's word with reverence, rejoicing and repetition; then watch how it will reward and guide you into living your dash to the fullest.

Mark 1:35 describes Jesus getting up early in order to go to a lonely place to pray. Most people who have developed a consistent quiet time with God have a set place to meet with God, a set time, and a set plan. Where is the best place for you to get alone with God, away from all the distractions of life?

_____

_____

_____

_____

What is the best time for you to consistently spend time with God, reading the Bible and praying? When are you at your best?

_____

_____

_____

_____

Do you have a consistent plan for reading your Bible and developing your relationship with God? If so, what is it?

_____

_____

_____

_____

_____

Living My Dash: Maintaining My Vision

God made it clear to me in the first few months of the new church plant that our vision was to start a purpose-driven church with the goal of reaching out to unchurched people in the community. Please note the words, clear to me. This vision was not clear to everyone attending. As I have already mentioned, some of the starter Christians came with their own agenda for the new church. Their desire was to build a church after their own image. Other people simply wanted to replicate a church exactly like the one from which I had just resigned. They were looking for a same song, second verse vision for the new church. As I began to share my new vision, some people began to question the whole idea of what they called "the purpose-driven model." This new model did not match their notions of the kind of church they wanted to plant.

This challenge became a wonderful opportunity for me to return to my study and to reexamine what the Bible really taught about the nature and purpose of the New Testament church. Following Nehemiah's example, I returned to the scripture for a fresh study to see if my vision for the new church was in line with the word of God. Were the concepts and principles taught by Pastor Rick Warren in his book, *The Purpose-Driven Church*, truly Biblical or was his concept just another here-today gone-tomorrow fad I had seen dozens of times in my ministry. Were the five purposes of God for the church promoted in this book nothing more the latest church planting fad, or were they truly God's vision for his church?

In his book, Pastor Warren made a strong case for the five purposes by combining the Great Commission and the Great Commandment. All five purposes are seen in these two important declarations by Jesus, but I wanted to see if the five purposes were found in other passages of scripture. I am suspicious of arbitrarily combining two scriptures together to prove a point, so I wanted to see if all five purposes could be found in a single text or in a single New Testament book. I opened my Bible and the search began.

> I wanted to see if the very first church practiced the five purposes of worship, fellowship, discipleship, ministry and evangelism...

I initiated my study in the Book of Acts. I wanted to see if the first century church possessed any or all of the purpose-driven qualities. I turned first to the second chapter of Acts, a historical section of scripture which described the birth of the church. Peter preached his famous sermon on the Day of Pentecost in the city of Jerusalem. At the conclusion of his message, around three thousand people accepted Christ and were baptized. The verses that follow in Acts 2:42-47 became the focus of my study. These verses are critically important to understanding the original purpose of the church. They are like a Polaroid snapshot of the early church before it had time to get off track. I wanted to see if the very first church practiced the five purposes of worship, fellowship, discipleship, ministry and evangelism described by Rick Warren. I challenge you to do the study for yourself. You will discover all five purposes were being practiced in the Jerusalem church.

I then turned to the planting of the Antioch Church described in chapters 11 and 13 of Acts. This passage describes the planting of the first Gentile Church. I wanted to know if this Gentile church would follow the same five purposes seen in the Jewish church. I was pleasantly surprised to discover all five purposes alive and well in the church at Antioch. So far, my study was substantiating the purpose-driven model. But I still was not satisfied. So I turned from the historical sections in Acts to the didactic, teaching sections in the New Testament letters. Would the letters confirm what I had discovered in Acts?

I found the same purpose-driven vision in the New Testament letters. Space does not permit a complete review of what I learned in my study, but suffice it to say, the five purposes are evident throughout the New Testament letters. One example: I remember preaching a series on The Book of Ephesians. In my preparation for the study, I discovered Ephesians covers all five purposes. In fact, Ephesians can be outlined using the five purposes. Do the study and here's what you will discover:

- Chapter 1: Worship
- Chapter 2: Fellowship
- Chapter 3: Evangelism
- Chapter 4: Ministry
- Chapters 5-6: Discipleship

I learned a valuable lesson through this experience. Fads come and go, and believe me when I say I have seen dozens float through the church in my years of pastoral ministry. But there is something different about the word of God. It is eternal and unchanging. It is timeless truth which will guide anyone's vision at any time in history. It was a return to the authoritative word of God that firmed up my vision and confirmed the direction of the new church. If the vision of your life purpose is centered and grounded in the Scripture, then your vision will be on target and stay on target.

During this reevaluation experience, I was reminded once again of how difficult it can be to maintain a vision. I recalled a true story I had heard when I was in college. A group of settlers landed on the northeast coast of America in the 1600's. The first year after they landed they began to lay out a town site. The second year they built the town. The third year they elected a city government. The fourth year the city government decided to build a road westward five miles into the wilderness.

Before the fifth year was completed, there was a movement to impeach the city government because the people said it was a waste of funds to go any further west. It is amazing how a group of people who could see 3,000 miles across an ocean could so quickly lose their pioneering vision that they could not see five miles across a continent.[13] The challenge is to intentionally and strategically keep the vision clear and compelling for the long haul.

Several years ago, Eugene Peterson wrote a superb book entitled, *A Long Obedience in the Same Direction*.[14] When I reflect on the challenges of fulfilling a life purpose, I wonder if that title should be tattooed on the arm of every believer who wants to finish a great work for God. That would include you. God has given you a vision for your life purpose. That is wonderful. But do not make the mistake of thinking that your vision will just maintain itself. There is no auto-pilot when it comes to fulfilling your life purpose. You must be willing to tenaciously grip the wheel and get ready for a long obedience in the same direction.

To successfully keep your life purpose on course, you need a dependable compass. Nehemiah leaves no doubt about the right course for his life. The only reliable guide is the word of God. It will keep you on track, focused on the goal and heading true north. But you must be willing to make the life-long commitment to maintain your vision by reading God's word with reverence, rejoicing and repetition. Do this and you will be on your way to successfully living your dash.

Living Your Dash

CHAPTER 6 – MAINTAIN YOUR VISION

Step #1: Read God's Word with Reverence (Nehemiah 8:1-8)

I will seek to listen to what God is saying to me as I hear His word, acknowledging that it is divinely inspired and authoritative. In my Bible reading, I will attempt to understand the author's original intention and apply God's truth to my life and circumstances, seeking help from wise teachers.

Step #2: Read God's Word with Rejoicing (Nehemiah 8:9-12)

Trusting that one purpose of scripture is to expose my sinfulness, I will respond to the conviction of the Holy Spirit with a repentant heart. I will be thankful for God's mercy and forgiveness. My joy will increase as I walk in greater freedom toward fulfilling my life purpose.

Step #3: Read God's Word with Repetition (Nehemiah 8:13-18)

I will develop a consistent habit of Bible study with the knowledge that God's word is truth. Like a compass, I will trust it to faithfully guide me toward true north in my journey to walk in His purposes for my life.

Father God,

The busyness of life often obscures my vision, and the noise of life keeps me from hearing your voice through the Bible. Help me develop the habit of reading your word and hiding it in my heart, so that I will discern your voice in this world. Like in the parable of the shepherd and his flock in John 10, I want to listen to your voice and know it, for your voice is trustworthy. Help me to walk in a long obedience in the same direction by reading your word with reverence, rejoicing and repetition.

In Jesus name I pray, Amen.

CHAPTER SEVEN

MAINTAIN YOUR BELIEFS

One of the most important distinctions I have learned in the course of reflection on Jewish history is the difference between optimism and hope. Optimism is the belief that things will get better. Hope is the faith that, together, we can make things better. Optimism is a passive virtue; hope, an active one. It takes no courage to be an optimist, but it takes a great deal of courage to have hope.

Jonathan Sacks

What comes to your mind when you hear the word *confession?* Perhaps it brings back memories of the time you were caught by your parents stealing coins from your brother's piggy bank and you had to admit your sin. Maybe it brings back dreadful memories when you were a teenager, waiting for your parents to arrive at the police station after the party you were attending was busted. You can still remember carefully rehearsing your statement as you awaited their arrival. Perhaps the memory of confession transports you back in time to sitting in a booth with a priest on the other side of the wall. If you are from a different religious tradition, confession may take you back to memories of walking down the aisle at the end of a sermon to acknowledge your sin. When I hear the word, I immediately think of sitting in the junior high school principal's office awaiting my sentencing for some mischievous prank I pulled.

What does the word confession mean in the Bible and how is it relevant to fulfilling your life purpose? The word literally means *to say the same thing, to agree with, to acknowledge.* For example, if I say to you, "I am driving a blue car," confession is basically agreeing with me and saying, "Yes, you are right. You are driving a blue car." In scripture it is essentially agreeing with the truth. To be more specific, it is agreeing with what God says is true. When God says something, confession is saying back to God, "Yes, God, you are correct. I am in total agreement with you."

We have now arrived at a pivotal step in sustaining your life purpose for the long haul and this critical step has everything to do with confession. This phase of the journey focuses on the importance of identifying your core beliefs and values, and what it takes to sustain them for the duration of your dash. What are your foundational beliefs, the unchanging principles and values that will guide your mission to the finish line? Circumstances will change along the way. Team members may come and go. Life is dynamic, so you can expect change. However, your core beliefs must never change. They must be based on the rock-solid truth of who God is, what he has done in history and what he has called you to accomplish during your dash. In your journey to complete your life purpose, your core beliefs will become critical foundation stones upon which your life mission is built. These core values must become a vital part of your lifelong confession. The core of confession is agreeing with God. This step will become the stabilizing foundation for the journey ahead because it is based on the solid and reliable truth of God's word.

Core beliefs are like the foundation of a house. The owner of a house can change many things in the structure: the color of paint, the type of flooring, the interior design. He can even move a wall or redesign the kitchen cabinets. But the owner never changes the foundation. To alter the foundation could damage the rest of the house. The core beliefs and values of your life mission will become the foundation upon which your life mission is built and will be sustained. As you will soon discover from the next section of Nehemiah's journal, your core values will grow out of the very nature of who God is.

What are the core beliefs you must declare as firm, fixed and non-negotiable? What are the values you will uphold with an inflexible and uncompromising commitment in your quest to fulfill your life mission?

What are some of your core beliefs that help guide your life?

_____

_____

_____

_____

_____

In chapters nine and ten in his journal, Nehemiah describes the core beliefs of his life mission. In a time of covenant renewal, Nehemiah and the Israelites confess their fundamental beliefs about God and about themselves. They agree with God on these vital truths. They not only subscribe to these core values; by the end of their declaration they actually sign in agreement on the dotted line to maintain them. From this great confessional statement, you can learn more than just a summary of the history of Israel. You can also discover the core beliefs and values you would be wise to proclaim and maintain as you travel on the road toward your life purpose.

Maintain Your Belief in God's Sovereignty (Nehemiah 9:1-6)

The public reading of God's word by Ezra and the Levites recorded in chapter eight leads the people to realize how far they have fallen as the People of God in keeping God's law. Reading the Biblical account of their early history and the story of their ancestor's rebellion against God is devastating to them. The good news is that the exposing light of God's word has done its work of revealing and exposing the fact that *"all have sinned and fall short of the glory of God"* (Romans 3:23).

Chapter nine begins with a corporate confession of sin by the people. It must have been a powerful moment for Nehemiah and the other leaders to witness this outpouring on the part of the people. It is as if God's word is bulldozing away centuries of sinful and rebellious rubble so that a new foundation can be laid. What comes next is a bold and dramatic confession given by the Levites. Their proclamation stands in stark contrast to their past sinfulness. They corporately declare the glorious sovereignty of God as the creator of the universe.

Listen to the great acknowledgement of God's sovereignty expressed by the Levites on behalf of all the people. *"Blessed be your glorious name, and may it be exalted above all blessing and praise. You alone are the Lord. You made the heavens, even the highest heavens, and all their starry hosts, the earth and all that is on it, the seas and all that is in them. You give life to everything, and the multitudes of heaven worship you"* (vv. 5-6).

The beginning stanza of this great confession is echoing the same truth taught long before Nehemiah's time by the great prophet Jeremiah. *"Ah, Sovereign Lord, you have made the heavens and the earth by your great power and outstretched arm. Nothing is too hard for you"* (Jeremiah 32:17). We must not miss the central point of this section of their proclamation. The underlying message to the Israelites is God has created something out of nothing; he has brought order and beauty out of chaos. He is a powerful God in sovereign control of all things. Therefore, he can be trusted to handle our difficulties and challenges in fulfilling our purpose on earth. There is great power unleashed when God's people gather together and publically proclaim his awesome power and sovereign control of the universe.

I still remember as a kid watching the Boston Celtics play under the leadership of the great coach Red Auerbach. Coach Auerbach had a routine which infuriated his opponents, but delighted his fans. It would happen toward the end of the game, if the Celtics had a comfortable lead. Red Auerbach would reach into his pocket, pull out one of his big cigars and light up. The fans would cheer enthusiastically because they knew this was the coach's way of saying, "We've got this game under control!" Now I'm not suggesting God smokes large cigars, but I am saying God can look down on our lives at any moment and regardless of the circumstances say, "I've got this one under control!"

Do you believe in the sovereignty of God as the creator and sustainer of the universe? Do you actually believe God is personally involved and in total control of this universe? Has the sovereignty of God become nothing more than just a religious statement in your church creed or is it one of the foundational beliefs and values upon which your life mission is built? Ask the New Testament writers this question and you will receive a clear and unequivocal answer. God is in sovereign control of all things and believers can stake their lives on it.

As an example of God's sovereignty, take a close look at the three great chapters in the New Testament which speak to the divinity of Jesus Christ. They are the first chapters in The Gospel of John, The Letter to the Colossians and The Letter to the Hebrews. These three great Chapter Ones reveal Jesus to be the creator and sustainer of the universe. As you read these passages, think of them as explanations of the specific job description of the second member of the Trinity, God the Son.

"In the beginning was the Word, and the Word was with God, and the Word was God. He was with God in the beginning. Through him all things were made; without him nothing was made that has been made" (John 1:1-3).

"He is the image of the invisible God, the first born over all creation. For by him all things were created: things in heaven and on earth, visible and invisible, whether thrones or powers or rulers or authorities; all things were created by him and for him. He is before all things, and in him all things hold together" (Colossians 1:15-17).

"In the past God spoke to our forefathers through the prophets at many times and in various ways, but in these last days he has spoken to us by his Son, whom he appointed heir of all things, and through whom he made the universe. The Son is the radiance of God's glory and the exact representation of his being, sustaining all things by his powerful word" (Hebrews 1:1-3).

There is no question concerning the truth these inspired writers are trying to convey in these three passages. Jesus Christ is none other than God the Son, and among his specific responsibilities as a member of the Trinity has been creating and sustaining the universe. He not only had the job of creating the universe. He now has the responsibility of holding the universe together, *"sustaining all things by his powerful word."* Scientists may prefer the word gravity to describe this phenomenon in our universe. Gravity is a helpful term to describe the fact that something is holding our universe together. However, these Biblical writers prefer a deeper explanation to describe what is keeping the universe from coming apart: *"in him all things hold together."* Just imagine the amount of power required to hold the entire universe together. This is the rather impressive scope and magnitude of Jesus' power.

Now to the reason why this is so important when it comes to your confession. Why do these New Testament writers agree with this same truth expressed in Nehemiah's declaration of the sovereignty of God over all creation? Why do they describe God as being both creator and sustainer of the universe? There is a significant so-what-difference-does-this-make behind their bold assertions. They want God's people to know and believe to the core of their being that God is in absolute and total control of all things; nothing is too difficult for him. This is the life-changing message we must learn from Nehemiah's confession: *If God can complete and sustain the creation of the universe, surely he can complete and sustain your life purpose!*

If you hope to live your dash to the fullest, you must believe unequivocally in the sovereign control of God in your life. He is in absolute control. The only question is, "Will you confess it?" The benefits of this declaration can be powerful in living your dash. You will worry less and trust more when you realize that nothing arrives in your life unless it first passes through the hands of your Heavenly Father. No matter what difficult or confusing circumstances you have to face, you can know that if God gets you to it, he will get you through it. This is why the Apostle Paul can assert with absolute assurance, *"Being confident of this, that he who began a good work in you will carry it on to completion until the day of Christ Jesus"* (Philippians 1:6). On the road to completing your life mission, maintain your belief in God's sovereignty.

> When life is challenging and appears to be out of control, to what degree do you trust in God's sovereignty? Explain.
>
> _____
>
> _____
>
> _____
>
> _____
>
> _____

Maintain Your Belief in God's Faithfulness (Nehemiah 9:7-8)

When God makes a promise, you can take it to the bank. Just ask Abraham. In the next part of Nehemiah's confession, he reflects back to the faithfulness God demonstrates in keeping his promise to Abraham, the father of Israel. *"You are the Lord God, who chose*

Abram and brought him out of Ur of the Chaldeans and named him Abraham. You found his heart faithful to you, and you made a covenant with him to give to his descendants the land of the Canaanites, Hittites, Amorites, Perizzites, Jebusites and Girgashites. You have kept your promise because you are faithful" (vv. 7-8).

The covenant promise God made to Abraham in Genesis 12:2-3 runs like a golden thread through the entire Bible. *"I will make you into a great nation and I will bless you; I will make your name great, and you will be a blessing. I will bless those who bless you, and whoever curses you I will curse; and all peoples on earth will be blessed through you."* The Biblical record that follows this promise is a testimony to the faithfulness of God to keep his word. God did bless Abraham and his descendants for generations to come.

But the implications of this promise go far beyond Abraham's immediate descendants. The Apostle Paul takes the fulfillment of God's promise to Abraham to an entirely new level in his letter to the Galatians that even has implications for Christians today. Paul sees this promise achieving its ultimate fulfillment in the coming of Jesus Christ, whom he describes as the seed of Abraham (3:16). As believers in Christ, we become children of Abraham by our faith and, therefore, recipients of the promise of Abraham (3:6-9). Sharing in this promise has for the believer in Christ both a privilege and a responsibility, just like it did for Abraham. The privilege is *I will bless you* and the responsibility is *you will be a blessing*.

> On the road to completing your life mission, maintain your belief in God's faithfulness.

The reality of being participants in the promise given to Abraham speaks directly into the finding and fulfilling of your life mission. You have been chosen by God to be his child and to receive blessings beyond measure. But you are also given the responsibility to be a blessing in the world by fulfilling God's plan and purpose for your life. God has made a new covenant with you through your faith in Jesus Christ and he will be faithful to keep his promise to bless you and to make you a blessing to others.

It is true: God has made a promise to be faithful to you. Do you believe that promise? Do you live in such a way that this promise is daily confessed as one of the unchanging beliefs of your life mission? You will find God to be utterly dependable and totally reliable to help you at every step of completing your life purpose. What God guides, God provides. This is no meaningless slogan for religious wall plaques. This is a reliable truth for all God's people to confess. On the road to completing your life mission, maintain your belief in God's faithfulness.

Describe ways that God has demonstrated his faithfulness to you in the past (maybe even in spite of your unfaithfulness).

_____

_____

_____

_____

_____

Maintain Your Belief in God's Power (Nehemiah 9:9-12)

I remember hearing Dr. James Dobson tell the humorous story about his son, Ryan, when he was just a toddler. There was a pick-up truck parked in their driveway with the tailgate down. Somehow, Ryan had managed to pull himself up onto the tailgate. But he was having trouble getting down. Dr. Dobson saw his son hanging halfway off the tailgate, his little legs dangling in midair. As Dr. Dobson approached his son to help him down, he could hear his son saying softly to himself, "Would somebody help this kid!"

In your journey to complete your life purpose, you can count on times when you will need to be rescued. So do the People of Israel. In this great confession, Nehemiah recalls times in Israel's national history when God comes to their rescue. *"You saw the suffering of our forefathers in Egypt; you heard their cry at the Red Sea. You sent miraculous signs and wonders against Pharaoh, against all his officials and all the people of his land...You divided the sea before them, so that they passed through it on dry ground, but you hurled their pursuers into the depths, like a stone into mighty waters"* (vv. 9-11).

What a powerful picture of how God loves to work on behalf of his people. Just when it looks as if Israel is finished, God shows up to save the day. This fact proven time and time again in Israel's history is worthy to be added to their confession. All my life I have heard people say, "God helps those who help themselves." They said it with such confidence and conviction that I was sure it was found somewhere in the Bible. I will save you the time and trouble of trying to find this verse. It is not there. But there are plenty of passages teaching the opposite truth: *God helps those who can't help themselves!* On the road to completing your life mission, maintain your belief in God as your ultimate and sufficient source of power.

This is what the Apostle Paul requests in his prayer recorded in the Letter to the Ephesians. Perhaps the believers in Ephesus were feeling insignificant and powerless. After all, they were a small group surrounded by the powerful and evil influences of the pagan culture of their city. Maybe this is why Paul prays that they would come to know *"his incomparably great power for us who believe. That power is like the working of his mighty strength, which he exerted in Christ when he raised him from the dead and seated him at his right hand in the heavenly realms"* (1:19-20).

Later in the same letter, Paul adds another request to his prayer. *"I pray that out of his glorious riches he may strengthen you with power through his Spirit in your inner being, so that Christ may dwell in your hearts through faith"* (3:16-17). He concludes his prayer with this assurance. *"Now to him who is able to do immeasurably more than all we ask or imagine, according to his power that is at work within us, to him be glory in the church and in Christ Jesus throughout all generations, for ever and ever! Amen"* (3:20-21).

The believers in Ephesus are not alone in feeling powerless and inadequate to meet life's challenges. We all have moments when we feel small, ineffective and incapable of making a difference for God. This is when the power of God must become part of your daily confession. You must maintain a strong and consistent belief in the power of God that is available for the completion of your life mission. Learn to lean into the power of God. You will find it eternally reliable.

Describe a time in the past when God demonstrated his power in your life.

_____

_____

_____

_____

_____

Maintain Your Belief in God's Love (Nehemiah 9:13-37)

There is in this section of the confession a cycle we hear repeated over and over again. God shows his love to the People of Israel by giving them his law to follow for their success; they decide to disobey God's law; God disciplines them for their sinful rebellion; Israel repents and cries out to God for deliverance; God forgives and restores Israel. Like a wheel rolling down the road of history, we see this cycle repeating itself throughout much of the Old Testament. We especially see this cycle during the era of the Judges and the Kings, the two historical periods which are referred to repeatedly in these verses in chapter nine of Nehemiah.

Notice how God's love is repeatedly described with two words: "You gave." God continually gave to Israel.

"You gave them regulations and laws that are just and right, and decrees and commands that are good" (v. 13).

"In their hunger you gave them bread from heaven and in their thirst you brought them water from the rock; you told them to go in and take possession of the land you had sworn with uplifted hand to give them" (v. 15).

"You gave your good Spirit to instruct them" (v. 20).

"You gave them kingdoms and nations, allotting to them even the remotest frontiers" (v. 22).

What an amazing picture of God's unconditional love. In spite of Israel's sinful and blatant rebellion, God's love is consistently unconditional and eternal. *"But you are a forgiving God, gracious and compassionate, slow to anger and abounding in love. Therefore, you did not desert them"* (v. 17). Even when Israel has to suffer the severe consequences of her sinful rebellion, there is never any doubt about God's underlying, sustaining love. *"But in your great mercy you did not put an end to them or abandon them, for you are a gracious and merciful God"* (v. 31).

You must understand that as a child of God, your failure is not fatal or final.

In your journey to complete your life purpose, there will be times when you, like Israel, fail to measure up to God's standards. You must understand that as a child of God, your failure is not fatal or final. God never stops loving you. He can't help himself. He is a good parent – the perfect parent – so he cannot ever stop loving his children. The Bible makes it clear that God is love. Love is at the core of his very nature and essence. Nothing you could ever do could change the nature and character of God. Even when your sinful actions result in punishment and painful consequences, God still loves you.

The great confession of Nehemiah acknowledges this truth and confesses it as one of the core beliefs of his life purpose. His example challenges us to do the same. We must never forget this great Biblical truth: *There is nothing you could ever do to make God love you more; there is nothing you could ever do to make God love you less!* God is love. Your heavenly Father truly is the God of new beginnings, second chances and do-overs. On the road to completing your life mission, maintain your belief in God's love.

> How has God demonstrated his unconditional love to you in spite of your dis-
> obedience and failures?
>
> _____
>
> _____
>
> _____
>
> _____

Nehemiah's beliefs proclaimed so powerfully on this occasion strike a chord in the hearts of the people. Their response is impressive as they agree with Nehemiah's confession, put it in writing and affix their seals to it. In other words, they sign on the dotted line to maintain these core beliefs and values as the Chosen People of God. Chapter ten provides an extensive list of the names of the individuals, especially the priests and leaders, who sign the covenant. The example of the leaders motivates the rest of the Israelites to join them in making this covenant with God. They even go so far as to bind themselves with a curse and an oath to obey God and follow his commandments. *"All these now join their brothers the nobles, and bind themselves with a curse and an oath to follow the Law of God given through Moses the servant of God and to obey carefully all the commands, regulations and decrees of the Lord our Lord"* (v. 29).

To make their commitment even more impressive, they immediately apply their pledge to three specific areas of their lives. First, they agree to apply God's truth to their marriages. They had been lax in the recent past in allowing their sons and daughters to marry unbelievers. Now they are ready and willing to correct this behavior. *"We promise not to give our daughters in marriage to the people around us or take their daughters for our sons"* (v.30). Nehemiah knows his history well. He recognizes that the root cause of many of Israel's problems throughout history could be traced back to the sin of compromise.

Years earlier, during the conquest of the Promised Land, Israel failed to obey God's clear instructions to totally destroy the idol-worshiping people in the land. Instead of following God's command, they allowed the evil influences to remain and were eventually drawn into idolatry. Nehemiah is wise to remind them of this historical fact and to highlight the direct connection between their poor choices and the painful consequences they are now enduring. *"But see, we are slaves today, slaves in the land you gave our forefathers so they could eat its fruit and the other good things it produces. Because of our sins, its abundant harvest goes to the kings you have placed over us. They rule over our bodies and our cattle as they please. We are in great distress"* (9:36-37).

We don't have to live long before we learn that poor choices have a way of leading to painful consequences. We really do reap what we sow. The only solution is the one offered by Nehemiah: a radical commitment to obey the commands of God and not compromise our values. The Apostle Paul would later challenge the Corinthian Church to make a similar commitment in the area of partnerships with unbelievers. *"Do not be yoked together with unbelievers. For what do righteousness and wickedness have in common? Or what fellowship can light have with darkness?"* (II Corinthians 6:14). On the road to fulfilling your life mission, watch out for the subtle temptation of compromise. It will land you in the ditch every time.

Second, they agree to apply God's truth to their business practices. They were guilty of blatantly violating various Sabbath laws commanded by God. Now they are ready to correct this behavior. *"When the neighboring peoples bring merchandise or grain to sell on the Sabbath, we will not buy from them on the Sabbath or on any holy day. Every seventh year we will forgo working the land and will cancel all debts"* (v. 31).

Here we see another example of how Israel's values had been compromised over the years by the subtle influence of unbelievers. It was easy for the Israelites to justify violating the Sabbath laws: What's the big deal with one day a week? This is the way business is done in the real world. We can't afford to take a day off. Compromising in what might be considered by some to be a small matter can quickly become a slippery slope that leads to disobeying God's law.

Third, they agree to apply God's truth to their finances. For years, they had neglected giving their tithes and offerings. Now they are ready to correct this behavior. *"We assume the responsibility for carrying out the commands to give a third of a shekel each year for the service of the house of our God… We also assume responsibility for bringing to the house of the Lord each year the firstfruits of our crops and of every fruit tree. As it is also written in the Law, we will bring the firstborn of our sons and of our cattle, of our herds and of our flocks to the house of our God, to the priests ministering there"* (vv. 32, 35-36). They continue in the verses that follow to enumerate a list of other tithes and offerings they will faithfully contribute to the house of God.

Getting serious with God leads the Israelites to get serious about their finances. The same will be true for you in living your dash. Your true priorities and values can usually be exposed by looking at two locations: your calendar and checkbook. How you spend your time and money will be like a window into what you truly value. Are you allowing God's truth to guide your financial decisions?

106

Choices. We all have to make them. The question is, will the choices we make be wise and move us closer to fulfilling our life mission? I don't know who first said these words, but the message is true:

There is a choice you have to make
In everything you do.
So keep in mind that in the end,
The choice you make makes you.

Israel's willingness to apply the truth of God's Word to their lives in such practical and specific ways is impressive. They make the right choices and these choices make them into a better people. They are willing to walk their talk by maintaining their core values and beliefs. It is easy to confess core values with your lips. The real challenge comes when you confess them with your life. Lip service or life service? This is the ultimate choice you face with your core beliefs.

> If people were to describe your core beliefs by examining only your calendar and checkbook, would they align with your stated core beliefs?
>
> _____
>
> _____
>
> _____
>
> _____
>
> _____

Living My Dash: Maintaining My Beliefs

I have learned two rules of thumb when building a church facility: *It takes twice as long to build as you anticipate and it costs twice as much as you hope to spend.* These two laws seem to be written in the rule book of church construction. I have witnessed these two laws at work every time I have led a church building project. The pattern is always the same. During the planning phase, a church building tends to grow as new ideas are conceived. What begins as a simple drawing on a napkin gradually expands until it becomes over time a large set of very expensive blueprints. The recurring phrase is repeated like the chorus of a church hymn: *This change-order will cost a little more, but it will be worth every dollar!* Multiply this by the number of people with new ideas – at least two ideas per church member – and you get the picture.

The construction of our Worship Center was no exception. Even though we tried to keep a lid on spending, the cost of the project seemed to increase exponentially every month, especially toward the end of the construction phase. The bank would only loan us a certain amount of money, so our building team quickly realized certain parts of the building project would have to be phased in later. For example, kitchens would be roughed in, but not completed. Cement patios and planter boxes would remain dirt. We did not even know for sure if we would be able to pave the parking lot. As for tables and chairs for classrooms... can you spell, "Sit on the floor!"

I knew God was in sovereign control of this project. He had proven his guidance and faithfulness to our young congregation time and time again through the fundraising and building design. He had demonstrated his love and leadership to us in a thousand ways. I had no doubt he had the power and resources to finish our building project in totality. However, when I checked the numbers, I could see only one clear reality: we did not have the necessary funds to finish the job. We would be able to move in, but in less than ideal circumstances.

Then something happened that changed everything. One day I received a call from a church member to let me know an elderly friend of hers had died. She had befriended this woman several years earlier. The woman had no living relatives, so our church member had felt led by God to take care of this aging lady and had done so for the last several years. It was not always a pleasant task because the woman was rather gruff and extremely frugal. I had met the lady only once when I was asked by the church member to drop in on her and pray with her. During our visit the lady told me she planned on including our church in her will. As I looked at the cheap furnishings in her low-income apartment, I thought to myself, "Great. We get to haul this stuff to the dump when she dies!"

One day I received the call that she died. I did not think any more about it until I received another call several days later from the church member. She said, "Rick, I have been cleaning out the lady's apartment. In sorting through her belongings, I am finding a lot of interesting papers. Apparently she had what seems to me to be a large amount of stocks and investments." That became the understatement of the year. Several months later when her estate was finally settled, the total was around $1.8 million. We were in fact one of three organizations listed in her will and received one-third of the estate, just over $600,000. With these additional funds, we were able to finish our Worship Center, including tables and chairs!

I would have never guessed in a million years that God would send the necessary funds to complete our building project through a person I had met only once and who had never attended our church. But when you are serving a God who is in sovereign control of the universe, who faithfully demonstrates his love to his children and is powerful enough to handle any challenge, anything is possible. This experience forever changed me. How could I ever again do anything less than confess the sovereign faithfulness and love of my powerful God. This is a belief I will maintain to the grave and beyond.

The next time you hear the word *confession*, I hope you will not think about parents, priests or your junior high school principal. I hope you will think about Nehemiah and the great confession he and Israel made about God. I hope you will think long and hard about the fundamental beliefs they confessed that day and how these core values helped guide them in very practical ways in completing their life purpose. I challenge you to maintain these same core values as you complete your mission: the values of God's sovereignty, God's faithfulness, God's power and God's love. Do this and you will be able to maintain your life purpose.

CHAPTER 7 – MAINTAIN YOUR BELIEFS

Step #1: Maintain Your Belief in God's Sovereignty (Nehemiah 9:1-6)
I will reflect upon the sovereignty of God as creator of the universe, acknowledging that he alone is Lord. God made the heavens, even the highest heavens and all their starry hosts, the earth and all that is on it, and the seas and all that is in them. God gave life to everything and gave purpose to my life. Because of this truth, I can trust that God is able to help me complete my purpose.

Step #2: Maintain Your Belief in God's Faithfulness (Nehemiah 9:7-8)
I will reflect on God's faithfulness to keep His promises. Just as God called Abram, changed his name and made a covenant promise to Abraham, God has chosen me and promises never to leave or forsake me. God is faithful to help me at every step of completing my life purpose.

Step #3: Maintain Your Belief in God's Power (Nehemiah 9:9-12)
God demonstrated His power to rescue the Israelites from captivity and to guide them through their wilderness journey. I will call upon God's power to help me in my struggles as I seek to fulfill my purpose.

Step #4: Maintain Your Belief in God's Love (Nehemiah 9:13-37)
God is a forgiving God, gracious and compassionate; slow to anger and abounding in love. Even when I fail to obey God, I know he will never stop loving me. Even when my sinful actions result in painful consequences, he still loves me because God is love. I will remember God's great love for me whenever I get discouraged while completing my life purpose.

Living Your Dash

Father God,

I acknowledge that you are the Sovereign God who created order and beauty out of nothing by speaking everything into existence. I am grateful for your faithfulness to rescue me and guide me by your power when I call on you. I am thankful for your abiding love which promises never to leave me or forsake me. Help me to apply these beliefs in practical ways through my relationships, in my daily life and with my finances so that I may bring honor and glory to your name.

In Jesus name I pray, Amen.

CHAPTER EIGHT

MAINTAIN YOUR GRATITUDE

I have learned that in every circumstance that comes my way, I can choose to respond in one of two ways: I can either whine or I can worship!
Nancy Leigh DeMoss

Piglet noticed that even though he had a very small heart, it could hold a rather large amount of gratitude.
A.A. Milne

Rudyard Kipling was so popular at one point in his career that his writings were getting ten shillings per word. A few college students, however, did not appreciate Kipling's writings. They devised a plan to poke fun at the writer. They sent Mr. Kipling a letter and enclosed ten shillings in the envelop, the going rate for one word. The letter read, "Please send us your best word." They received a letter back from Kipling with a single word, "Thanks."

Is *thanks* one of your best words? When you hear the word *thanks*, what immediately comes to your mind? Do you think of a holiday celebrated annually or an attitude practiced daily? Being thankful can easily slide down the list of priorities if you are not careful. I heard about a husband who bought his wife a beautiful skunk coat for Christmas. When his wife opened the gift, she said, "I cannot see how such a nice coat could come from such a foul smelling little beast." Her husband responded, "Hey, I don't ask for thanks, but I do demand respect!"

What is on your gratitude list? An anonymous mother wrote the following list of things for which she was grateful:

■ For automatic dishwashers. They make it possible to get out of the kitchen before the family comes in for their after-dinner snacks.

■ For husbands who attack small repair jobs around the house. They usually make them big enough to call in professionals.

■ For the bathtub. It's the one place the family allows Mom some time to herself.

■ For children who put away things and clean up after themselves. They are such a

111

joy you hate to see them go home to their own parents.

- For gardening. It is a relief to deal with dirt outside the house for a change.
- For teenagers. They give parents an opportunity to learn a second language.
- For smoke alarms. They let you know when the turkey is done.

Ask Nehemiah about the importance of gratitude, and he will be the first to say, "Let's push gratitude back to the top of the priority list." This is exactly what he does after the great covenant renewal described in chapters nine and ten is completed. The Israelites have wholeheartedly renewed their commitment to be fully devoted followers of God. They have drawn a line in the sand, declaring themselves to be the Chosen People of God. They have promised on oath to live holy and godly lives in honor of their God. Nehemiah is now ready to lead them to the next step in their journey, the step of gratitude.

In chapter 12 of his journal, Nehemiah declares a day of thanksgiving for the purpose of dedicating the completed wall around Jerusalem. When we think of dedication services today, we tend to envision a brief ceremony, including a short speech and perhaps the presentation of a bronze plaque, followed by cake and punch. This is nothing like the ceremony Nehemiah is planning. Nehemiah's plans are big because he is preparing a celebration to honor a big God.

Nehemiah begins by inviting some of the key leaders who will be involved in leading the celebration. *"At the dedication of the wall of Jerusalem, the Levites were sought out from where they lived and were brought to Jerusalem to celebrate joyfully the dedication with songs of thanksgiving and with the music of cymbals, harps and lyres. The singers were also brought together from the region around Jerusalem"* (v. 27-28). Nehemiah is obviously planning a huge celebration to honor God and to express his heartfelt gratitude to God for the successful completion of the wall.

Why is it so significant to remember Nehemiah's emphasis here concerning the importance of gratitude? In living your dash, do you really need to invest the time and expense of planning celebrations along the way? Is it that important to occasionally hit the pause button and gather your team together just to celebrate? Wouldn't you be a better steward of your time and money if you just forged ahead to complete your life mission? These are all important questions to ask during the long-term maintenance phase of living your dash.

I have learned from experience as a leader that it is absolutely essential to pause at critical times in the journey and celebrate. I have to admit that I did not understand the value of celebration as a young leader. My tendency was to focus too much on arriving at the destination and not enough on enjoying the journey. My attitude was, "Let's get the project completely finished. Then we will blow up the balloons and have cake and punch."

Nehemiah corrects this attitude with a much healthier plan. We will discover in the next chapter that Nehemiah's work is not done. There is much more to be completed in the maintenance phase of his life mission. We will see his still-to-do-list when we get to the final chapter of his journal. However, in chapter 12, Nehemiah says to his team, "It's time to stop and celebrate. It's time to express our gratitude to God for what he has accomplished."

In your journey to find and fulfill your life purpose, there will always be a temptation and tendency to forge ahead with the goal of completing the project. But something unhealthy will happen to you and your team if you fail to schedule times of celebration. You will lose your attitude of gratitude. It will not be intentional, but accidental. As time passes and the excitement fades, so does gratitude. Add to this the reality of obstacles and opposition along the way, and before long you will find yourself filled with grumbling, not gratitude. If you don't schedule times of celebration, you will soon lose the joy of the journey. Fulfilling your life mission will become a drudgery to be endured instead of a delight to be enjoyed.

Like Nehemiah, you will need to intentionally schedule special times to say to God, "Thanks for helping me reach this point in my journey. Thanks for letting me live my dash with meaning and purpose. And thanks for helping me build a great support team." This kind of intentional gratitude will force you to remember what God has done in your past. Otherwise, you will forget to remember what God has already done. You will only see what still needs to be done and fail to see what has already been accomplished. Once again, Nehemiah can be your guide. You can learn from Nehemiah's celebration service some valuable pointers on how to maintain your gratitude.

> What consumes most of your contemplations and conversations: grumbling or gratitude? Why?
>
> _____
>
> _____
>
> _____
>
> _____

Celebrate With Purification (Nehemiah 12:27-30)

The first action for Nehemiah and his team is to ceremonially purify themselves for the celebration service. *"When the priests and Levites had purified themselves ceremonially, they purified the people, the gates and the wall"* (v. 30). The purpose behind this purification ceremony is to focus their whole lives on being grateful to God, recognizing that the success of their completed construction project is totally dependent on God's favor. This kind of focused purification does not just happen. It takes dedication and a concentrated effort to decide to be wholly set apart to honor and praise God in thanksgiving.

The word pure is used to describe something that is unmixed, undiluted or uncontaminated. To celebrate God with gratitude demands that you remove anything that would pollute, contaminate or spoil your attitude of thanksgiving. Do you ever allow unhealthy, negative attitudes to infiltrate your heart and mind so that the priority of thanksgiving is compromised? Learning to identify these enemies of gratitude is essential to successfully living your dash. A gratitude that is authentic and pure demands that the following three deadly attitudes have to go.

First, worry has to go. How can you be thankful to God for yesterday if you cannot trust him to provide for tomorrow? Worry will absolutely destroy gratitude in your life. We know this from the teachings of Jesus. Are you aware that one of the longest sections in the Sermon on the Mount is dedicated to the topic of worry? In Matthew 6:25-34, Jesus warns his followers of the crippling effects of worry. Jesus describes worry as:

- **Unnecessary**: *"Look at the birds of the air; they do not sow or reap or store away in barns, and yet your heavenly Father feeds them."*
- **Unbecoming**: *"Are you not much more valuable than they [the birds]?"*
- **Unproductive**: *"Who of you by worrying can add a single hour to his life?"*
- **Unfaithful**: *"If this is how God clothes the grass of the field, which is here today and tomorrow is thrown into the fire, will he not much more clothe you, O you of little faith. So do not worry."*

Worry will suck the joy and gratitude out of living. This is why Jesus concludes this section on worry with a strong admonition. *"Therefore, do not worry about tomorrow, for tomorrow will worry about itself. Each day has enough trouble of its own."* God knows this to be true, so he requires that worry has to go. Perhaps it would help Christians not to worry if they realized Jesus' words are in the imperative. Jesus is not suggesting that his followers not worry. He is commanding them to not worry. Jesus has good reason to place this non-negotiable requirement on his followers. He knows the irreparable damage worry can have in a person's life. In your journey to complete your life mission, worry has to go.

Second, complaining has to go. How can you be grateful to God for what he has already provided if you spend your time and energy complaining about what he has not provided? I am always fascinated at how certain commands in the Bible are conveniently overlooked by some Christians. A great example is the imperative of Philippians 2:14-15. *"Do everything without complaining or arguing, so that you may become blameless and pure, children of God without fault in a crooked and depraved generation, in which you shine like stars in the universe.*" Notice the passage does not say, Do most things or Do some things. It actually says, "Do everything without complaining or arguing."

How can Christians read this simple, straightforward command from God and still spend hours complaining and arguing? What is really sad is that much of the complaining and arguing is directed toward God. Instead of taking time to express gratitude to God, people spend their time complaining about their circumstances and arguing with God about the way he is running the universe.

According to these verses, having a complaining and argumentative attitude will undoubtedly prevent Christians from ever becoming blameless and pure, and will significantly impede their influence in the world. God has strategically placed Christians in this crooked and depraved world and it is their responsibility to shine like stars. There is no way Christians can complain to God and shine for God at the same time. This is why complaining has to go.

Third, pride has to go. How can you express gratitude to God if you are busy congratulating yourself and taking credit for what you have accomplished? Pride is the antithesis of gratitude because it turns the spotlight on you instead of God. The goal of gratitude is the exact opposite in that it places God in the spotlight he deserves.

This was one of the tragic mistakes made by Israel after they entered the Promised Land. They forgot to remember that all the blessings and provisions in their new home were gifts from God. But they had no excuse for their spiritual amnesia. Moses had warned them repeatedly of this danger before they ever crossed the Jordan River and set foot in their new homeland.

We see these warnings in The Book of Deuteronomy, which is a collection of speeches given by Moses to the Israelites as they prepare to enter the land. The 40 years of wilderness wanderings are finally complete and the obstinate generation is dead and gone. Now it is time for a new day, a new leader and a new generation in Israel's history. However, before Moses officially hands the baton of leadership over to Joshua, he has some final worlds of instruction and warning for the new generation.

In these speeches, Moses continues to present the same admonition: *"Don't forget to remember!"* Read through these powerful speeches recorded in Deuteronomy and you hear the words, *remember, do not forget*, repeated on almost every page. Listen to the introductory words to The Book of Deuteronomy. *"In the fortieth year, on the first day of the eleventh month, Moses proclaimed to the Israelites all the Lord had commanded him concerning them"* (Deuteronomy 1:3). The word *proclaimed* in this verse is actually the word *engraved*. Moses wants Israel to engrave onto their hearts and minds the lessons of the past so they will always remember and never forget what God has done for them.

In one of his most powerful and pointed speeches recorded in Deuteronomy eight,

115

Moses gives the following caution. *"You may say to yourself, 'My power and the strength of my hands have produced this wealth for me.' But remember the Lord your God, for it is he who gives you the ability to produce wealth, and so confirms his covenant, which he swore to your forefathers, as it is today"* (8:17-18).

Tragically, Israel did not listen to Moses' admonition. It was just a matter of time before pride took over and pushed God off the throne. The end result of their pride historically was the destruction of Jerusalem and the Babylonian Captivity. Pride is the natural enemy of gratitude, so pride has to go.

President Abraham Lincoln gave a similar warning to Americans in his day. He delivered his Proclamation for a National Day of Fasting, Humiliation and Prayer on April 30, 1863. He proclaimed, *"We have been the recipients of the choicest bounties of heaven. We have been preserved, these many years, in peace and prosperity. We have grown in numbers, wealth and power, as no other nation has ever grown. But we have forgotten God. We have forgotten the gracious hand which preserved us in peace and multiplied and enriched and strengthened us; and we have vainly imagined, in the deceitfulness of our hearts that all these blessings were produced by some superior wisdom and virtue of our own. Intoxicated with unbroken success, we have become too self-sufficient to feel the necessity of redeeming and preserving grace, too proud to pray to God that made us! It behooves us, then to humble ourselves before the offended Power, to confess our national sins, and to pray for clemency and forgiveness."* [15]

What a great reminder to regularly and consistently purify yourself before your Maker. Learn to ask yourself, "Am I truly grateful to God? Am I totally giving my undivided attention to developing the habit of being thankful? Have I allowed worry, complaining or pride to pollute and spoil my attitude?" Paul said it best in I Thessalonians 5:18. *"Give thanks in all circumstances, for this is God's will for you in Christ Jesus."* I talk to people all the time who struggle with knowing God's will for their lives. They say, "I just don't know what God's will is for my life. If God would reveal his plan for my life, I know I would be happy."

Maybe you have said something similar in your own search for God's plan for your life. If so, don't miss the point of Paul's message to the Thessalonians. You may not know every detail of God's purpose for your life, but this verse makes one fact perfectly clear: gratitude is a vital part of the will of God for you. God loves a grateful heart, so in your search for God's purpose and plan for your life make it a daily practice to give thanks with a pure heart.

Are you living your dash with a pure heart? Have you allowed contaminants like faithless worry, negative complaining or self-sufficient pride to pollute your attitude? It is no accident that Nehemiah begins the dedication celebration by leading the people in a purification ceremony. However, behind the outward ceremony there is the inward reality.

Nehemiah's desire is for the people to genuinely purify themselves before God from the heart. Purification always begins with the heart. Jesus said, *"Blessed are the pure in heart, for they will see God"* (Matthew 5:8). How's the condition of your heart? Purify your heart and who knows, maybe God will show up more often. In your life purpose journey, don't forget to celebrate with purification.

What process of purification do you need to encounter in your life today to enable you to become more grateful to God?

_____

_____

_____

_____

_____

_____

Celebrate With Preparation (Nehemiah 12:31-39)

It is impressive to observe all the planning and preparations that go into the dedication service. There is nothing sloppy or careless about the preparations for this celebration. Nehemiah and his leaders give great attention to the details of every aspect of the service. The singers, choirs and instrumentalists are trained, rehearsed and directed. The processionals for the dedication service are carefully programmed to proceed along the top of the newly built wall around the city of Jerusalem. Nothing is left to chance. Use your imagination to picture the pomp and ceremony of this great event. Nehemiah recalls, *"I had the leaders of Judah go up on top of the wall. I also assigned two large choirs to give thanks. One was to proceed on top of the wall to the right... The second choir proceeded in the opposite direction. I followed them on top of the wall, together with half the people"* (vv. 31, 38).

I grew up in a church where this kind of preparation in worship was a foreign concept. The only person genuinely prepared on most Sunday mornings was the preacher, and on some Sundays, I even had my doubts about his preparation. Every other part of the service involved little or no preparation. Words like sloppy, careless and unprepared could be used to describe most of our Sunday assemblies. I remember on many occasions seeing the song leader sitting on the front pew selecting songs from the hymnal five minutes before the service was to begin. During the same five minutes, the head usher was rushing around trying to find enough volunteers to pass the communion trays and offering baskets. When the song leader had finally selected his songs for the morning, he quickly went in search of someone to lead the morning prayer. And we wondered why the Sunday services lacked excitement and vitality.

There is no excuse for being sloppy when it comes to worshiping God. You don't see Nehemiah's song leader sitting on the front row, picking out hymns five minutes before the service. You don't see him rushing around hoping to find willing singers and instrumentalists to lead the music. Our God is a great God and he is worthy of our highest praise. Does he always receive this quality of praise? How many times does he receive nothing more than half-baked worship from his people? I realize the danger of over-planning to the point of losing all spontaneity. However, we must never call it spontaneous when in fact it is just lazy and sloppy.

I remember seeing a cartoon picturing a Sunday morning service at the First Church of the Barely Committed. On top of the communion table were a piece of stale bread and a cup of watered-down grape juice. Carved into the front of the communion table were these words: This'll have to do in remembrance of him. Something is tragically wrong when God receives worship that is careless and unplanned.

I am married to a great worship leader, so I know what it takes to celebrate with preparation. I see it every week. My wife spends hours in prayer and preparation for every single Sunday service. She always wants to carefully read over my sermon and text for a given Sunday, which means I have to have the rough draft of my sermon to her at least two weeks in advance. She then selects songs that will complement the message so that the hearts of the people will be prepared to listen to God's word. Once the songs are selected, the music is distributed to the singers and instrumentalists well in advance so they can learn their parts before the one-hour weekly rehearsal on Wednesday evening. Finally, the musicians arrive early on Sunday morning for another one-hour rehearsal before the actual service. This is just the routine for the weekly service. You should see the planning and preparation required for Christmas and Easter!

Nehemiah has every reason to celebrate in thanksgiving, probably more than any other person present that day. He knows he is witnessing nothing less than a mighty miracle of God. As he looks at the completed wall surrounding the city, Nehemiah is well aware that this is without a doubt a great work of God. Nehemiah would be the first to admit that he is no builder. He has no contractor's license, no trained construction crew and no experience building walls. He is a cupbearer for King Artaxerxes. Ask him about wine and he is your man. But building a wall? You better look elsewhere for your answers. However, Nehemiah does have something in his favor. He has a vision from God to build a wall and he knows God has allowed him to finish the task. Nehemiah is celebrating with a grateful heart because he has the privilege of living his dash to the glory of God.

There now stands before his eyes this magnificent wall. There is only one reasonable explanation: *God did it. God built the wall.* At the beginning of the project, the critics said the wall could not even hold up a fox. Now it is holding up the People of God. Can you see it? Nehemiah can. Only God can do something like this, a God worthy of highest praise and heartfelt thanksgiving. With God's help, nothing is impossible. This kind of God deserves more than lazy worshipers and sloppy planning. He deserves our noblest preparation. In your life purpose journey, don't forget to celebrate with preparation.

What are some specific ways that you can be more prepared to worship and celebrate God?

_____

_____

_____

_____

_____

Celebrate With Participation (Nehemiah 12:40-47)

The time finally arrives for the dedication service to begin. Everyone takes their places. *"The two choirs that gave thanks then took their places in the house of God; so did I, together with half of the officials"* (v. 40). Then we notice something interesting. Nehemiah makes it clear that this dedication service is not to be a one-man show. It is not designed to be an up-front performance by the professionals. Yes, leaders are leading, directors are directing and instrumentalists are playing. But notice also that all the people are participating. Even the women and children are playing a vital role in this celebration service. *"And on that day they offered great sacrifices, rejoicing because God had given them great joy. The women and children also rejoiced"* (v. 43). I love that last line. When God's people gather to celebrate God's goodness, there is a place for everyone.

What about all the people who do not have musical skills and talents? Not everyone has musical gifts. Is there a special role for the non-musicians to play in celebrating God's goodness? The final section of chapter 12 provides the answer. The non-musicians celebrate in the gift of giving. Nehemiah points out how all the people, including the non-musical people, do their part in financially supporting the full-time staff musicians. *"So in the days of Zerubbabel and of Nehemiah, all Israel contributed the daily portion for the singers and gatekeepers. They also set aside the portion for the other Levites, and the Levites set aside the portion for the descendants of Aaron"* (v. 47). This is how important thanksgiving is to Nehemiah and his team. He wants everyone involved in some way in praising God.

I have had the wonderful privilege of attending a number of events sponsored by Promise Keepers, a Christian organization with the goal of challenging men to be fully devoted followers of Jesus Christ. Words cannot express what it is like to gather in outdoor stadiums with tens of thousands of Christian men from all over the nation, from every conceivable denominational background, for the single purpose of worshiping God together. The events are always filled with great speakers and great times of fellowship. But the highlight for me is the music. To hear 50,000-plus men raise their voices in praise to God is enough to raise the dead, spiritually speaking.

I remember one such gathering in Boulder, Colorado. At one point during the praise time, the worship leader said, "Let's give a loud shout of praise to God so that the entire city of Boulder can hear how much we love God." The men began to shout, 50,000 strong. The volume grew and grew until we finally ran out of air. I thought later that this must have been similar to the sound of rejoicing at Nehemiah's celebration. *"The sound of rejoicing in Jerusalem could be heard far away"* (v. 43).

In John 10:10, Jesus says, *"The thief comes only to steal and kill and destroy; but I have come that they may have life, and have it to the full."* I am afraid that for many Christians, Satan has stolen the joy of singing. They enjoy listening to others sing, but for whatever reason, they do not join in and sing. This is especially alarming to me when I see Christian men sitting through the Sunday morning praise time, but not singing. I know some don't sing because they are convinced they don't sing well enough to join in. For others, Satan has deceived them into thinking that singing is not manly and is something for the women and children. What a diabolical deed Satan has done in robbing Christians, especially Christian men, of the life-transforming joy of praise through singing.

I challenge Christian men everywhere to break free from this lie from Satan and begin to enjoy the benefits of obeying the command of Scripture to sing.

"Speak to one another with psalms, hymns and spiritual songs. Sing and make music in your heart to the Lord, always giving thanks to God the Father for everything, in the name of our Lord Jesus Christ" (Ephesians 5:19-20).

"Let the word of Christ dwell in you richly as you teach and admonish one another with all wisdom, and as you sing psalms, hymns and spiritual songs with gratitude in your hearts to God" (Colossians 3:16).

120

If you are thinking these Scriptures are a command for all God's people and not just for a select few with special musical gifts, you are correct. Why not begin to enjoy the liberating benefits of obeying God's command and begin to sing this coming Sunday.

Worship is not designed to be a spectator sport. It is fully participatory. Even for those who cannot carry a tune in a bucket, they can still make a joyful noise. In addition to singing, they can contribute financially so that people called by God to be worship leaders can dedicate their full-time attention to planning and leading God's people in celebration. There are no exemptions in thanksgiving. Everyone needs to be engaged and involved.

Many years ago two young men were working their way through Stanford University. At one point their money was almost gone, so they decided to engage the great pianist Paderewski for a concert and use the profits for board and tuition. Paderewski's manager asked for a guarantee of $2,000. The students worked hard to promote the concert, but they came up $400 short. After the performance, they went to the musician, gave him all the money they had raised, and promised to pay the $400 as soon as they could. It appeared that their college days were over. "No, boys, that won't do," said the pianist. "Take out $1,600 for all your expenses, and keep for each of you ten percent of the balance for your work. Let me have the rest."

Years passed. Paderewski became premier of Poland following World War I. Thousands of his countrymen were starving. Only one man could help. He was the head of the U.S. Food and Relief Bureau. Paderewski's appeal to him brought thousands of tons of food. Later he met the American statesman to thank him. "That's all right," replied Herbert Hoover. "Besides, you don't remember, but you helped me once when I was a college student."

The moral of the story is a simple one: great things happen when everyone participates. Paderewski did his part to help two struggling college students. Later, Herbert Hoover was able to do his part to help meet the need of Paderewski. It is the same with living your dash. God never intended life to be lived in isolation. We are better together. In your life purpose journey, don't forget to celebrate with participation.

What changes need to take place in terms of your participation in the celebration of God?

_____

_____

_____

We must also remember that worship for Christians is not to be limited to what they do one hour on Sunday. Sunday celebrations are essential, but not exhaustive for believers. Worship is something they do all the time. As participants in the New Covenant, the challenge for all believers is to become lifelong worshipers of God. *"Therefore, I urge you, brothers, in view of God's mercy, to offer your bodies as living sacrifices, holy and pleasing to God – this is your spiritual act of worship"* (Romans 12:1). Worship for the Christian is much more than just one hour on Sunday. True worship is the daily giving of oneself to the purposes of God and is to involve all the time the Christian lives, everywhere the Christian goes and everything the Christian does. This definitely includes the times Christ followers gather for corporate worship and praise. Allow the Sunday celebrations to charge your spiritual batteries for a week-long experience of worship as you offer yourself in service to the purposes of God.

Let corporate worship experiences become times of great celebration in your life as you celebrate with purification, preparation and participation. *"Let us not give up meeting together, as some are in the habit of doing, but let us encourage one another – and all the more as you see the Day approaching"* (Hebrews 10:25).

Follow the example of Nehemiah in returning gratitude to the top of your priority list. Make it a point to regularly get together with fellow believers so that you can encourage one another and be thankful for God's blessings. Make the decision to live your dash everyday with an attitude of gratitude. You will never regret it.

Living My Dash: Maintaining My Gratitude

I was excited the day the leader of my building team called me and said, "Rick, I just found a piece of property that might be just what we need." He picked me up at our rented office and we drove to the property. I loved the location. It was just what we needed, even though I did not really know exactly what we needed at the time. We discovered it was an old, 22-acre alfalfa farm on the north edge of town.

The previous church I helped plant owned five acres, so this parcel seemed too large. My thought was this piece of property might work for us. We could keep the acreage needed for our facilities and sell off the rest of the property to help defray the cost. It was not long before we purchased the property for a great price. Once we built our Worship Center, we were ready to decide what to do with the unneeded acreage.

We wanted to make sure we did not make any mistakes at this point in our journey, so we hired an architectural firm to prepare a master plan of the property. Hiring this firm was one of the best decisions we ever made. We shared with them our future dreams and goals as a church, and they drew on paper the buildings we would need to make it happen. After several meetings with their team of architects, I shared with them my original idea to sell off some of the property so that we could pay down our building loan. I asked them, "How many acres do we need to sell?" They suddenly had a puzzled look on their faces and said to me, "Sell? Are you kidding? You will need every square inch to take care of the future buildings, parking, landscaping and required drainage."

I had forgotten about the city code requiring a designated amount of property for landscaping and drainage. The architects then rolled out the master plan for us to see. They were not kidding. We would need every square inch of the 22-acres to meet our future goals.

A year or so later, I was attending a conference and heard a pastor speak who was from a small town in Southern California. He was leading a purpose-driven church in a smaller city very much like ours, so I immediately felt a connection with him. In the course of his message, he mentioned that his church had reached ten percent of their community for Christ. When I heard this part of his story, my heart almost jumped out of my chest. I thought, "That's what I want to do for God. I want our church to reach ten percent of Roswell for Christ so that at the Second Coming of Jesus, we can present a tithe of our city to God!"

As I began to let this thought percolate in my mind, it suddenly dawned on me, "What if we don't have enough property to build the necessary buildings to reach ten percent?" When I returned home from the conference, I pulled out a calculator and the master plan from our architects, and started to crunch the numbers. When I finished doing the math, I sat in my office stunned. Using the proposed master plan with all the future buildings, landscaping, drainage and parking, we would have just enough room to take care of ten percent of our community in two Sunday morning services.

I wish I could take credit for this perfect master plan, but all credit goes to another Master Planner who is perfect in all his ways. From the first day we drove out to see the property, God knew the end from the beginning. While we sat in the car and dreamed that day, God had already master planned our property so we could someday reach our goal. Now honestly, with a God who pulls off this kind of miracle, there is only one way for me to live out the rest of my dash: with gratitude.

How high on your list of priorities is thanksgiving? I assure you that gratitude is still at the top of my list and will be until the day I die. I am living the remainder of my dash with a grateful heart. Nehemiah is challenging you to move gratitude to the top of your priority list, too. Following Nehemiah's example of purification, preparation and participation, the sound of rejoicing in Jerusalem could be heard far away. Who knows the impact your life purpose may have on others as they witness you giving thanks to God. Maintain your gratitude and you will be living your dash in a way that pleases God.

Living Your Dash

CHAPTER 8 – MAINTAIN YOUR GRATITUDE

Step #1: Celebrate With Purification (Nehemiah 12:27-30)

I understand the importance of showing gratitude to God for His work in my life. In order to celebrate God with gratitude, I will remove anything that would pollute, contaminate or spoil my attitude of thanksgiving. Rather than being filled with worry, complaining, or pride, I will express my thankfulness to God for His work in my life.

Step #2: Celebrate With Preparation (Nehemiah 12:31-39)

Showing gratitude to God through worship means that I must come prepared to worship. I will seek to be more prepared for times of corporate worship by getting a good night's rest, focusing my mind's attention and heart's affection upon God, and not allowing others to distract me from corporate worship.

Step #3: Celebrate With Participation (Nehemiah 12:40-47)

I understand that corporate worship is never to be a spectator sport. I will seek to find ways to become more engaged in worship through singing, praying, leading, and sharing my gifts and talents with others.

Father God,

I am truly grateful for your leadership in helping me fulfill my life purpose. Please forgive me for the times I have failed to show gratitude and to focus in worship. Help me approach times of corporate worship with more attention to being spiritually prepared through repentance of my sins. Help me come prepared mentally, emotionally, spiritually, and physically to engage fully in worship.

In Jesus name I pray, Amen.

CHAPTER NINE

MAINTAIN YOUR INTEGRITY

Who is wise? One who can tell what will be hatched from the egg that has been laid. Not he who can see the future – that is a prophet. Wisdom is seeing tomorrow's consequences of today's events.
Babylonian Talmud, tractate Tamid

Do not be deceived: God cannot be mocked. A man reaps what he sows.
The Apostle Paul

If you ever have the opportunity to fly over the Statue of Liberty, you will be impressed with the details on the top of Lady Liberty's head. The sculptor, Frederic Auguste Bartholdi, did a painstaking job with her coiffure. But he must have been certain that once the statue was secured on its pedestal, no one would ever see his attention to detail, except maybe for sea gulls flying overhead.

The Statue of Liberty was dedicated on October 28, 1886. At this time in history, Bartholdi could never have dreamed that any human being would ever fly over his statue. The Wright Brothers did not succeed in getting their plane airborne until December 17, 1903, a flight lasting only 12 seconds and covering a mere 120 feet. It would be years before planes had the power and ability to fly over the Statue of Liberty. And yet, Bartholdi finished off this hidden part of his masterpiece with as much care as he had devoted to her face, her arms or her torch. He finished the job, even in the areas where he thought no one would ever see. Such was this man's commitment to excellence and a virtue called integrity.[16]

Someone has said, "Integrity is what you have when no one is looking." We get the word integrity from the root word integer, which means whole or complete. From the same root, we get the word integrate, which means to pull various parts together into one united whole. The antonym is disintegrate, meaning to take something that is whole and break or pull it apart.

Are you a person of integrity? How do you live when no one is looking? Do you live a divided life or a united life? Do you act one way at church and another way at home or work? Is there a great divide between your behavior around your Christians friends and

125

the way you act with non-Christians? How about out-of-town trips? Are you like a chameleon, always changing colors to fit your surroundings? Are you a modern-day Dr. Jekyll, Mr. Hyde? How do you live when no one is looking? Are you a person of integrity?

The closing chapter of Nehemiah's journal provides a bold challenge to pull yourself together into a fully integrated person so that you can live out the remainder of your dash with consistency and character. Nehemiah knows that a life mission without integrity is a crash looking for a place to happen. But what does living with integrity look like in the real world? Chapter thirteen explains how and why it is critical that you live the rest of your dash by maintaining your integrity.

What does a life of integrity look like to you?

_____

_____

_____

_____

_____

Maintain Your Integrity among Evil Influences (Nehemiah 13:1-9)

I'm sure you have heard the old expression, "While the cat is away, the mice play." Something like this happens in Jerusalem during a period of time when Nehemiah is out of town. You will recall from chapter one that Nehemiah had first left Babylon for Jerusalem in the twentieth year of King Artaxerxes, 444 B.C. (cf. 1:1). The events of chapter 13 take place in the thirty-second year of King Artaxerxes, 432 B.C. (cf. 13:6). This means Nehemiah and the residents of Jerusalem are now 12 years into the maintenance phase of their project.

We know from our study so far that great things happen in Jerusalem during the first part of this 12-year stretch. The wall is completed in spite of many obstacles and much opposition. Under the leadership of Ezra and Nehemiah, the people renew their commitment to be fully devoted followers of God and pledge to be obedient to his law in such areas as marriage, keeping the Sabbath and financial stewardship. Vows are made and covenants are signed. The wall is then dedicated during a special assembly of God's people, filled with processions and music, a celebration of praise and thanksgiving devoted to God for all he has accomplished for and through his people.

Now we turn the clock forward 12 years. Several toxic changes begin to take place in Jerusalem that are cause for alarm. There is slippage in the commitments the people had made to God years earlier. Time has passed since the renewal of their vows to God. Now they are failing to maintain their integrity. Duplicity is creeping in and is gradually eroding their spiritual devotion to God.

To make matters worse, Nehemiah has left Jerusalem and returned to King Artaxerxes, so he does not know anything about these lethal events. However, when he returns to Jerusalem and discovers what has been happening in his absence, he is furious. Once again this great leader has to take the bull by the horns and correct these problems.

The first problem Nehemiah encounters involves a priest in Jerusalem by the name of Eliashib. While Nehemiah had been out of town, Eliashib had the audacity to clean out one of the large temple storerooms and let a rather unsavory character move in. *"Before this, Eliashib the priest had been put in charge of the storerooms of the house of God. He was closely associated with Tobiah, and he had provided him with a large room formerly used to store the grain offerings and the incense and temple articles, and also the tithes of grain, new wine and oil prescribed for the Levites, singers and gatekeepers, as well as the contributions for the priests. But while all this was going on, I was not in Jerusalem, for in the thirty-second year of Artaxerxes king of Babylon I had returned to the king. Sometime later I asked his permission and came back to Jerusalem. Here I learned about the evil thing Eliashib had done in providing Tobiah a room in the courts of the house of God"* (vv. 4-7).

You probably remember the name Tobiah from earlier pages in Nehemiah's journal. Tobiah is the Ammonite who opposed Nehemiah from the very beginning and tried to prevent the rebuilding of the wall (cf. 2:10). Along with Sanballat the Horonite and Geshem the Arab, Tobiah formed the axis of evil opposing Nehemiah's every move. Tobiah had been accurately identified by Nehemiah as an enemy of God.

I know what you are probably thinking at this point in the story. How could a person like Tobiah, who is an enemy of God, end up with free lodging in the house of God? Plus, Tobiah is an Ammonite and God's Law strictly forbids Ammonites from being allowed into the assembly of God's people. *"No Ammonite or Moabite or any of his descendants may enter the assembly of the Lord, even down to the tenth generation. For they did not come to meet you with bread and water on your way when you came out of Egypt, and they hired Balaam... to pronounce a curse on you"* (Deuteronomy 23:3-4; cf. Nehemiah 13:1-3). Can you imagine Nehemiah's shock and horror when he finds Tobiah the Ammonite living inside the temple courts? How could something like this ever happen?

Nehemiah explains the root cause of Eliashib's serious error in judgment. *"He was closely associated with Tobiah"* (v. 4). Don't read over those words too quickly. Eliashib's integrity is compromised and his judgment is severely impaired because he is hanging out with the wrong crowd. His close association with Tobiah leads him to make a disastrous decision. Such is the power of evil influences.

Before you throw too many rocks at Eliashib, take an honest look in the rearview mirror of your own life. How damaging would you say evil influences have been in your past? Could you tell similar horror stories of irresponsible decisions you have made simply because you were too closely associated with bad influences? Could you also describe how some of your stupid decisions eventually resulted in you having to pay stupid tax? You must always be careful with your close associations. Always ask, "Am I influencing others or are they influencing me?" Peer pressure does not clear up when your face does. It is a lifelong challenge you must face and conquer.

This leads to an important question concerning the long-term maintenance of your integrity. How should you deal with evil influences which have the power to negatively affect the overall outcome of your life mission? Let Nehemiah once again be your teacher and example. Take good notes as you watch his quick and decisive response. He quite literally takes matters into his own hands. *"I was greatly displeased and threw all Tobiah's household goods out of the room. I gave orders to purify the rooms, and then I put back into them the equipment of the house of God, with the grain offerings and the incense"* (vv. 8-9). How's that for taking decisive action? Nehemiah takes all of Tobiah's household goods, throws them out and fumigates the place.

There is a powerful and essential lesson in the way Nehemiah handles this first challenge. You may have to terminate some evil influences in your life for the sake of your integrity. Evil influences have a subtle way of gaining a foothold. Once established, they can do irreparable damage to you and to the success of your life mission. Remember what the Bible say about evil influences.

- *"Evil companionship corrupts good morals."*
- *"A little leaven leavens the whole lump."*
- *"Avoid the very appearance of evil."*
- *"If it causes you to sin, cut it off."*

The Bible does not mince words concerning the dangers of evil influences and neither should you. Identify the evil influences in your life and make a decision to avoid them. I heard the story about a man who went in to see his doctor. He said, "Doctor, I broke my arm in three places. What should I do?" The doctor said, "Stay out of those three places!" What are the places you should avoid? Who are the people you need to avoid? What relationships do you need to terminate? These decisions may be painful to make, but they must be made for the sake of the integrity of your life purpose. Otherwise, duplicity will destroy your integrity.

What evil influences do you need to remove from your life in order to maintain your integrity?

_____

_____

_____

_____

_____

Maintain Your Integrity in Giving (Nehemiah 13:10-14)

I said earlier if you want to know your true priorities in life, you need only check two places: your calendar and your checkbook. Where you invest your time and money reveals what is most important in your life. Jesus wisely observes, *"For where your treasure is, there your heart will be also"* (Matthew 6:21). It is always a challenge to maintain integrity in the area of giving. There are so many excuses you can use to justify your ungenerous attitude, such as: "We've had extra expenses this month; we were out of town last Sunday; we are trying to recover from spending too much at Christmas; let the pastor get a real job!"

The Tobiah-living-in-the-temple incident is not the only problem Nehemiah encounters when he returns to Jerusalem. He also discovers the people are slacking off in their offerings. *"I also learned that the portions assigned to the Levites had not been given to them, and that all the Levites and singers responsible for the service had gone back to their own fields. So I rebuked the officials and asked them, 'Why is the house of God neglected?'"* (vv. 10-11). Nehemiah has to be wondering how something like this could happen. The Israelites had made a vow back in chapter ten to give their offerings and to provide for the Levites and singers. But now they are slacking off and not maintaining their vow. We have already learned that vision leaks; so does commitment.

Their disobedience in the area of giving not only has a negative effect on the ministry at the temple. Their actions also make it necessary for the temple singers to be laid off. Since the offerings are so low, the full-time staff has to get other jobs. No wonder there is ample room for Tobiah the Ammonite to live in the temple storeroom. That storeroom is supposed to be filled with their tithes of grain, new wine and oil.

God's ministry and God's ministers always suffer when people do not maintain integ-

rity in giving. According to most surveys in recent years, the majority of church members in America do not tithe. The majority of studies are in agreement that the average percent of giving in American churches is usually around three to four percent. I will always remember the conversation I had one day with a perspective church member. He asked me if we practiced the modern tithe. I said, "I have never heard the term. What is the modern tithe?" He answered, "It is five percent." I responded, "At our church, we call that one-half of a tithe!" Can you imagine what local churches could accomplish for the Kingdom of God if every member tithed? What would happen if church members started to faithfully tithe and church budgets suddenly tripled. Do you think the Great Commission might be accomplished and the Gospel of Jesus Christ would finally go into the entire world?

Practicing integrity in giving is a huge hurdle for many Christians. I heard the story of a Christian lady who inherited a large sum of money. She wanted to give a portion of the inheritance to God, but she could not decide how much to give. The longer she waited and the more she debated with herself, the more difficult it was to give. She finally made her decision and said to God, "God, I am going to take all the money I inherited and throw it into the air. Whatever you want, you keep. Whatever falls to the ground will be mine!"

The good news is that the people of Israel respond positively to Nehemiah's rebuke. *"All Judah brought the tithes of grain, new wine and oil into the storerooms"* (v. 12). Nehemiah then puts in place some new policies and procedures to prevent this kind of disaster from happening again. He wisely selects a small group of leaders to oversee the offerings and temple storerooms. These individuals are handpicked by Nehemiah *"because these men were considered trustworthy"* (v. 13).

Christians today would do well to follow Judah's example. Do not play games with God when it comes to giving. The prophet Malachi says that failing to give tithes and offerings is nothing short of robbing God. *"'Will a man rob God? Yet you rob me.' But you ask, 'How do we rob you?' 'In tithes and offerings. You are under a curse — the whole nation of you — because you are robbing me. Bring the whole tithe into the storehouse, that there may be food in my house. Test me in this,' says the Lord Almighty, 'and see if I will not throw open the floodgates of heaven and pour out so much blessing that you will not have room enough for it'"* (Malachi 3:8-10).

God is the giver of all good gifts. Everything belongs to him. He gave you what you have and he can take it back anytime he wants. It could be that he wants to pour out a greater blessing on you, but he is holding back the blessing because you are holding back your tithes and offerings. You will never go wrong by maintaining your integrity in giving.

131

What changes, if any, do you need to make in your giving to exercise true integrity?

_____

_____

_____

_____

_____

_____

_____

_____

_____

_____

Maintain Your Integrity at Work (Nehemiah 13:15-22)

Old habits die hard. This is certainly the case with the Israelites and the keeping of the Sabbath. If you recall, the people made a vow to God back in chapter ten to refrain from working or even selling on the Sabbath. But now they are back to their old bad habits and are compromising their vow. *"In those days I saw men in Judah treading winepresses on the Sabbath and bringing in grain and loading it on donkeys, together with wine, grapes, figs and other kinds of loads. And they were bringing all this into Jerusalem on the Sabbath. Therefore I warned them against selling food on that day"* (v. 15).

Apparently the temptation to make a little extra money is just too much for some in Jerusalem. Working on the Sabbath seems like a small price to pay for an increase in income. The lure for more money entices them to violate their promise to God. They fail to maintain their integrity at work.

In your life purpose journey, there will always be the temptation to compromise your integrity on the job. It is so easy to let moral standards and Biblical ethics slide in order to make a quick buck or to fit in with the crowd.

In his book, *UnChristian*, David Kinnaman reports the following: *"In virtually every study we conduct, representing thousands of interviews every year, born-again Christians fail to display much attitudinal or behavioral evidence of transformed lives. For instance, based on a study released in 2007, we found that most of the lifestyle activities of born-again Christians were statistically equivalent to those of non-born-agains. When asked to identify their activities over the last thirty days, born-again believers were just as likely to bet or gamble, to visit a pornographic website, to take something that did not belong to them, to consult a medium or psychic, to physically fight or abuse someone, to have consumed enough alcohol to be considered legally drunk, to have used an illegal, non-prescription drug, to have said something to someone that was not true, to have gotten back at someone for something he or she did, and to have said mean things behind another person's back. No difference."* [17]

What kind of impact can your life purpose have if people see no difference in the way you live? The answer is, "No difference!" Nehemiah sees the seriousness of this problem and quickly moves to correct it, even to the point of getting physical. *"If you do this again, I will lay hands on you"* (v. 21). You can be sure this *laying on of hands* is not for ordination. Perhaps strangulation, but not ordination! How ruthless and determined are you to be a model of integrity at work? Will you be guided by the Almighty God or the almighty dollar? If people see no difference in you at work, you will make no difference in their lives.

Why does Nehemiah get so worked up about the Jews working on the Sabbath? A clue to answering this question may be found in verses 17-18. *"I rebuked the nobles of Judah and said to them, 'What is this wicked thing you are doing – desecrating the Sabbath day? Didn't your forefathers do the same things, so that our God brought this calamity upon us and upon our city? Now you are stirring up more wrath against Israel by desecrating the Sabbath.'"* What is the calamity Nehemiah is referring to and what does it have to do with this generation of Jews living in Jerusalem?

The prophet Jeremiah may provide some needed insight. In Jeremiah 17:19-27, the prophet assures the residents of Jerusalem that God will bless and protect them if they keep the Sabbath. Jeremiah assures them, *"But if you are careful to obey me, declares the Lord, and bring no load through the gates of this city on the Sabbath, but keep the Sabbath day holy by not doing any work on it, then kings who sit on David's throne will come through the gates of this city with their officials. They and their officials will come riding in chariots and on horses, accompanied by the men of Judah and those living in Jerusalem, and this city will be inhabited forever"* (vv. 24-25). Jeremiah paints an attractive picture of God's protection and provision when Israel keeps the Sabbath.

However, Jeremiah warns of tragic consequences if they decide to violate the Sabbath laws. *"But if you do not obey me to keep the Sabbath day holy by not carrying any load as you come through the gates of Jerusalem on the Sabbath day, then I will kindle an unquenchable fire in the gates of Jerusalem that will consume her fortresses"* (v. 27).

The calamity Nehemiah is referring to is the destruction of Jerusalem by the Babylonians in 586 B.C. Of course, there were other reasons for God allowing the destruction of Jerusalem and the captivity of his people, namely idolatry, wicked kings and corrupt priests. However, it is noteworthy that one of the reasons behind the destruction of

Jerusalem is the fact that Israel repeatedly and blatantly violated the Sabbath. Jeremiah's prediction of the burning of the gates of Jerusalem became a reality when the Babylonian armies invaded the city. The description of the fall of Jerusalem recorded in II Chronicles 36:21 provides an interesting and almost eerie insight into the importance of keeping the Sabbath. *"The land enjoyed its sabbath rests; all the time of its desolation it rested, until the seventy years were completed in fulfillment of the word of the Lord spoken by Jeremiah."* It is as if the land had been robbed of its rest because of Sabbath violations, so God is allowing the land a season of divine restitution so it can enjoy its rightful rest.

I find it interesting that years later, one of the main repairs Nehemiah and the workers have to complete on the wall construction is the rebuilding of the gates because, as Nehemiah observes, they had been *"burned with fire"* (Nehemiah 1:3; cf. 2:13). Obviously, God is serious about us taking a day off every week.

Speaking of work, have you learned how to not work? Have you learned the importance of taking a day off? Let's not miss the obvious point Nehemiah is making. Taking a day off every week is a command of God. I realize Christians have been debating the Sabbath for years and have disagreed as to exactly how it is to be applied to Christians. However, can we at least agree on one application? God says we all need a once-a-week break from the job.

This especially applies to you in your quest to finish the work God has given you in fulfilling your life mission. The subtle temptation is to rationalize – *What I am doing is ministry. It is more than just a job. My life mission is so important that I'm sure it makes me exempt from taking a Sabbath break each week. Besides, I don't know how much more time is left in my dash. I have things to do, places to go and people to see. This is no time to be taking breaks.*

Nehemiah takes exception to this argument. He is obviously involved in a great work of God and time is of the essence, but he still takes a day off to rest, reflect and refresh. Go back and read the Ten Commandments in chapter five of Deuteronomy. You will find no exemption clauses in the command to keep the Sabbath. The truth is God created us and knows our limitations. He understands how we are wired. He has designed us in such a way that we function optimally when we schedule regular breaks.

My experience is that Christian pastors and leaders are some of the worst offenders in this area. They fill up their calendars and leave no room for margin, thinking they are immune to fatigue and burnout. Is it any wonder that so many pastors leave the ministry every year? Just because a person's work is also a person's ministry is no excuse for violating God's universal principle of work and rest. Nehemiah knows the Jews in Jerusalem are no exception to the rule and neither are you. If you want your life purpose to impact others for the long haul, you must be determined to maintain integrity in your work.

What changes do you need to make to maintain your integrity at work?

_____

_____

What changes do you need to make in your schedule so you can take a day off every week?

_____

_____

_____

Maintain Your Integrity in Marriage (Nehemiah 13:23-31)

The Apostle Paul gives a stern warning in I Corinthians 6:14. *"Do not be yoked together with unbelievers. For what do righteousness and wickedness have in common? Or what fellowship can light have with darkness?"* Nehemiah would give a hearty "Amen!" to Paul's admonition. He seems to be facing a similar challenge with the Israelites. *"Moreover, in those days I saw men of Judah who had married women from Ashdod, Ammon and Moab. Half of their children spoke the language of Ashdod or the language of one of the other peoples, and did not know how to speak the language of Judah. I rebuked them and called curses down on them. I beat some of the men and pulled out their hair. I made them take an oath in God's name and said, 'You are not to give your daughters in marriage to their sons, nor are you to take their daughters in marriage for your sons or for yourselves'"* (vv. 23-25).

God has always given serious warnings to believers concerning the danger of marriage to unbelievers and for good reason. God knows what usually happens. The unbeliever influences the believer toward impurity and compromise. Again we see duplicity replacing integrity in the life of the believer.

Nehemiah uses Solomon as his prime example of the danger of making compromises in the area of marriage. Solomon may have been the wisest man to ever live, but he failed to follow his own advice in the area of marriage. Tragically, this mistake led to his downfall. *"Was it not because of marriages like these that Solomon king of Israel sinned? Among the many nations there was no king like him. He was loved by his God, and God made him king over all Israel, but even he was led into sin by foreign women"* (v. 26).

135

Nehemiah's commentary on the downfall of Solomon is dead-on accurate. Like Nehemiah, Solomon was chosen by God for a special life mission. Solomon was given the awesome privilege and responsibility of building the Jerusalem Temple. He was successful in completing this part of his life mission. However, he failed miserably to maintain his spiritual integrity throughout the rest of his life.

It all started with a single compromise when he married an unbeliever. *"Solomon made an alliance with Pharaoh king of Egypt and married his daughter. He brought her to the City of David until he finished building his palace and the temple of the Lord, and the wall around Jerusalem"* (I Kings 3:1). It would be easy to rationalize Solomon's behavior as nothing more than a strategic political move on his part. Besides, this was the way international politics worked in his day. All the other kings did it. But that was the core of the problem. Solomon was getting his cues from the pagan nations instead of the word of God.

Tragically, Solomon's tendency to compromise in the area of marriage went from bad to worse. The downward spiral is described in graphic detail in the eleventh chapter of II Kings. *"King Solomon, however, loved many foreign women besides Pharaoh's daughter — Moabites, Ammonites, Edomites, Sidonians and Hittites. They were from nations about which the Lord had told the Israelites, 'You must not intermarry with them, because they will surely turn your hearts after their gods.' Nevertheless, Solomon held fast to them in love. He had seven hundred wives of royal birth and three hundred concubines, and his wives led him astray. As Solomon grew old, his wives turned his heart after other gods, and his heart was not fully devoted to the Lord his God, as the heart of David his father had been"* (vv. 1-4).

Integrity is all about being fully devoted. The end of Solomon's life is one of duplicity, not integrity. What a sad story of a man who began with such promise, but finished in utter failure. Nehemiah is wise to hold Solomon up as an example of how not to live in the area of marriage.

The reality of Christians compromising their integrity by marrying unbelievers is epidemic today. I have lost count of how many times I have seen this kind of compromise destroy the integrity of Christians. It generally comes in three phases.

Phase 1: **Rationalization** – *"I know after we are married, I can change him/her."*

Phase 2: **Conflict** – *"Now that we are married, we cannot agree on spiritual issues like church attendance, giving, morals and values."*

Phase 3: **Compromise** – *The believer, in order to keep peace at home, drops out of church and falls away.*

Nehemiah and Paul leave no doubt about how a believer is to maintain integrity in marriage. Do not marry an unbeliever. Better to be single than miserable. If you are a Christian who is married to an unbeliever, the answer is not to run out and get a divorce. Paul provides a better path for you to follow (see I Corinthians 7). However, if you are single, heed God's warning. The person you marry must *"belong to the Lord"* (I Corinthian 7:39). Whatever it takes, do not compromise here. Maintain integrity in your marriage. Your life purpose will be greatly stifled if you are unequally yoked in marriage with an unbeliever.

> What changes do you need to make to maintain your integrity in marriage?
>
> _____
>
> _____
>
> _____
>
> _____

How are you doing in maintaining your integrity in these four areas: evil influences, giving, work and marriage? Are you feeling the strong pull to compromise? Resist it. The story is told that when Mark Twain left the Mississippi river boats, he became a reporter in Carson City, Nevada. From there he wrote a letter to an old friend that Carson City was "a den of booze, wild women and twenty-four hour gambling. Certainly no place for a good Presbyterian... so I no longer am one!" The pressure will be on you as a Christian to no longer be one. Do not give in to the pressure. Do not compromise. Maintain your integrity to the end.

Living My Dash: Maintaining My Integrity

I have seen my share of Christian leaders wreck their life purpose, some in the national news and others in the town where I live. How does it happen? How can a Christian leader with so much potential lose it all by falling into sin? The answer is simple: it happens one compromise at a time. Start compromising your integrity in the little things, and before long you will find yourself sliding down the slippery slope of sin. After seeing more than enough Christian leaders destroy their reputation and integrity, I decided that was one tee-shirt I did not want to someday own. So I determined to take Nehemiah's advice to heart and to be ruthless in protecting my integrity.

I clearly saw the warning in the Bible. David prayed, *"Teach me your way, O Lord, and I will walk in your truth; give me an undivided heart, that I may fear your name. I will praise you, O Lord my God, with all my heart; I will glorify your name forever"* (Psalm 86:11-12). The words undivided heart and all my heart jumped off the page. I knew this described the life of integrity. It dawned on me that there was one common denominator I witnessed in all the fallen Christian leaders: duplicity. There is great danger in trying to live a double life. God wants a whole, undivided heart of integrity.

Perhaps this is why Jesus spent so much of his time exposing hypocrisy and condemning disingenuous religion. Perhaps this explains Jesus' caustic words addressed to the teachers of the law and the Pharisees of his day. *"Woe to you, teachers of the law and Pharisees, you hypocrites! You are like white-washed tombs, which look beautiful on the outside but on the inside are full of dead men's bones and everything unclean. In the same way, on the outside you appear to people as righteous but on the inside you are full of hypocrisy and wickedness"* (Matthew 23:27-28). I understood the great danger in duplicity. I knew I did not want my life purpose to be derailed by this subtle enemy. But how could I protect my integrity all the way to the finish line?

I live just over an hour from the Sierra Blanca ski resort. One winter day, a friend and I headed up the mountain for a day on the slopes. It was a beautiful sunny day and the skiing was superb. However, toward the end of the day a storm moved in and dumped about a foot of fresh snow. This was great for skiing, but not so great for the drive to the bottom of the mountain. The road from Sierra Blanca is narrow and winding, with plenty of sharp curves. Miss one of these curves, and the drop off is severe.

The descent that day was especially slippery and dangerous. Our car fish-tailed around every turn on the slick icy pavement. However, my friend and I were greatly comforted by the presence of guardrails. At the dangerous curves, guardrails had been installed to prevent a vehicle from heading over the edge. Not one time was I tempted to say to my friend, "I hate those guardrails. They block the scenic view!" Just the opposite was true. I wanted to personally nominate for sainthood whoever installed them. Those protective pilings served an important role which was to keep our vehicle on the road so we could make it safely to our destination.

We all need spiritual guardrails in our lives. We need to build into our daily routines some kind of protection to keep us on the road to fulfilling our life purpose. The temptations are legion in the world today, so we must have the tenacity of Nehemiah to guard our integrity. After seeing so many promising Christian leaders go over the edge, I decided to build into my life some spiritual guardrails. The protective barriers you need may not exactly match mine, but perhaps the following four suggestions will at least give you a starting point.

First, I guard who I am. It is essential that I be the same person no matter where I am. I cannot be one person in the pulpit, another person at home and still another person sitting in front of my computer. Integrity demands that I get my act together and avoid

138

a life of duplicity. I must accept the person God made me to be and not ever try to be anything or anyone other than me, both in public and in private.

Living a divided life is exhausting because it means that I must constantly hold up a mask in front of the real me. And the mask has to be changed depending on which group I am with at any given time. Living with integrity allows me to be the same person, regardless of who I am with at the time. I am able to relax and be the person God created and called me to be.

Second, I guard where I go. There are some places where I just don't need to go, some events I need not attend because temptation is too strong. There was a time in my life when I would have seen this as a sign of weakness. But I have done a total reversal on this one. It is not a sign of weakness to admit a weakness. Rather, it is a sign of strength to say, "This is a place I need to avoid."

This means that people who struggle with alcohol don't need to frequent bars. People who struggle with pornography need to put a filter on their computer. Where are the places you need to avoid? Are you strong enough to admit your areas of weakness? The Apostle Paul said, "When I am weak, then I am strong" (II Corinthians 12:10). Never be afraid of humbly admitting an area of weakness. The future success of your life purpose is worth the humility.

Third, I guard who I am with. This guardrail requires a great deal of honesty and evaluation. The goal is not to run and hide in a Christian convent so there will be no contact with people. This guardrail is more about developing a wise discernment with the people I am around.

For example, I am very careful about being alone with a woman. I don't have lunch meetings or even drive in a car alone with a woman. Nehemiah taught me the danger of rumors, so I try not to fuel any rumors about my integrity. I am also very cautious in avoiding negative people who gossip and cause division. The Apostle Paul said in Romans 16:17, *"I urge you, brothers, to watch out for those who cause divisions and put obstacles in your way that are contrary to the teaching you have learned. Keep away from them."* Those are rather strong words, but Paul says to keep away from such people, so I do.

Fourth, I guard what I see. The old warning from the computer world applies equally to our spiritual lives: Garbage in, garbage out. Put a filter on what you let into your mind. Romans 12:2 says, *"Do not conform any longer to the pattern of this world, but be transformed by the renewing of your mind. Then you will be able to test and approve what God's will is — his good, pleasing and perfect will."* Since I am being transformed by the renewing of my mind, I want to keep my mind as uncluttered as possible. Otherwise, I could easily miss out on God's will for my life mission.

Are you serious about the danger of compromise? Have you allowed subtle influences to contaminate your whole-hearted devotion to God? Think of your life as a load of laundry. The first thing you do before you wash a load of clothes is separate the whites from the darks. You never have to worry about the whites fading onto the darks. It is always the other way around. Your concern is always that the darks will fade onto the whites. Be on your guard against any evil influences that might contaminate the purity of your life.

My wife and I have been married over 35 years. I can honestly say I have never been tempted to be unfaithful to her. This is not because I am so spiritual that I am beyond temptation. I am convinced it is because I have carefully and intentionally erected spiritual guardrails that steer me clear of the very appearance of evil. It's really not rocket science. I will never go over the cliff if I stay away from the edge. Sure, this limits where I go, who I am with and what I see. But the reward of fulfilling my life purpose and maintaining my integrity to the finish line is worth the sacrifice. I try to operate with this simple rule of thumb in every decision I make, every place I go and everything I do. I call it my Sunday Pulpit Rule: *Would I feel comfortable sharing this from the pulpit this Sunday?*

How serious are you about maintaining your integrity? Are you determined to be disciplined, and even ruthless, when compromise comes knocking at your door? Believe me, it will come knocking – with evil influences, in your giving, at work and even in your marriage. Maintaining your integrity may be the toughest challenge you will ever face in fulfilling your life purpose, but it can also be the most rewarding. The rewards will make it all worthwhile.

You will notice that Nehemiah prays three times in chapter 13.

- *"Remember me for this, O my God, and do not blot out what I have so faithfully done for the house of my God and its services"* (v. 14).
- *"Remember them, O my God, because they defiled the priestly office and the covenant of the priesthood and of the Levites"* (v. 29).
- *"Remember me with favor, O my God"* (v. 31).

Nehemiah's prayers reflect the heart of a man passionate about integrity. He cares deeply about maintaining the integrity of the things of God, whether it is about the house of God or about the priests who minister there. I especially appreciate the final prayer. *"Remember me with favor, O my God."* God obviously answers Nehemiah's prayer. In fact, God remembers him with such favor that he preserves the story of his life purpose in the pages of Scripture. Not bad for an exiled cupbearer from Babylon without a contractor's license! Maintain your integrity to the very end, and just like Nehemiah, God will be able to remember you with favor.

Living Your Dash

CHAPTER 9 – MAINTAIN YOUR INTEGRITY

Step #1: Maintain Your Integrity among Evil Influences (Nehemiah 13:1-9)
I understand that bad company corrupts good morals. Therefore, I will guard my closest relationships and ensure that my closest friends are on the same path that I desire to walk.

Step #2: Maintain Your Integrity in Giving (Nehemiah 13:10-14)
I will demonstrate financial integrity and good stewardship by obeying God with a tithe of all that I make. I will give the first ten percent of my income to God through my local church.

Step #3: Maintain Your Integrity at Work (Nehemiah 13:15-22)
I understand the importance of demonstrating consistency in my Christian walk regardless of my setting. I will show integrity at work by maintaining the same values and morals as I do at church or home.

Step #4: Maintain Your Integrity in Marriage (Nehemiah 13:23-31)
I trust that God's plan for me is the best plan, especially when it comes to marriage. I will obey God by only dating people who are Christians actively pursuing a love relationship with God.

Father God,

Thank you for giving Jesus as a perfect example of integrity in every aspect of life. I also thank you for giving the Holy Spirit who guides me in living a life of integrity. Give me wisdom and direction to demonstrate a life of integrity in my friendships, giving, work and marriage. Forgive me for the times when my integrity fails, and help me learn from my mistakes. Continue to show your strength in my weaknesses.

In Jesus name I pray, Amen.

CONCLUSION

Too many people are having what we call "near-life experiences." They go through life bunting, so afraid of failure that they never try to win the big prizes, never knowing the thrill of hitting a home run or even taking a swing at one.
Charles Parnell

Dream as if you'll live forever; live as if you'll die today.
James Dean

So ends the amazing story of the cupbearer from Babylon who has a passionate vision to build a wall around Jerusalem. But this is no ordinary vision. This is a vision inspired and fueled by a God big enough to pull off the impossible. That is, big enough to pull off the impossible *if.* God is big enough if Nehemiah is willing to take the risk. God has always been looking for men and women who are willing to take a risk. He likes to call it *faith.* God is a real believer in faith. In fact, it is impossible to please God without it (Hebrews 11:6). But in order to have a faith that is ready to risk, we must be willing to overcome the fears that impede.

Henry Ford said, *"One of the greatest discoveries a man makes, one of his greatest surprises, is to find he can do what he was afraid he couldn't do."*

I wonder if Nehemiah was ever afraid he could not build the wall. I wonder if at the end of a long day he ever collapsed on his bed, doubting if he could overcome all the obstacles and complete his God-given task. The *if* word is a big little word and has the power to paralyze the best of us. I would bet there were plenty of days when Nehemiah felt dreadfully untrained and overwhelmed, extremely intimidated and outnumbered, and completely inadequate for the task ahead.

You can expect to have the same doubts and fears on your journey to find and fulfill your life mission. There will be days when the task before you seems too much to handle, the challenges too great to overcome, and the opposition too strong to conquer. Like the Jewish spies in the Promised Land, you will feel like grasshoppers compared to the giants which must be defeated.

It is at these moments I hope you will remember the life lessons you have learned from a cupbearer named Nehemiah. In spite of insurmountable odds and overwhelming

142

obstacles, he begins a journey of finding and fulfilling his life purpose. And by the grace of God, he arrives at his destination and pulls off the impossible.

I am often challenged by the humorous words penned by an anonymous writer called "Cautious Man."

There was a very cautious man
Who never laughed or played.
He never risked, he never tried
He never sang or prayed.
And when he one day passed away
His insurance was denied.
For since he never really lived,
They said he never died! [18]

In his book, *Who Switched the Price Tags*, Anthony Campolo references a very unique sociological study conducted several years ago. What makes the study so unique is that it was conducted with 50 people over the age of 95. They were asked one question: "If you could live your life over again, what would you do differently?" It was an open-ended question, allowing these elderly people to answer in unstructured ways. As you might guess, there was a wide range of answers. However, three answers continued to emerge and dominated the results of the survey: If I had it to do over again, I would reflect more, I would risk more and I would do more things that would live on after I am dead. [19]

This sounds like a commentary on the life of Nehemiah. His life mission story begins as he reflects on the dreadful condition of the inhabitants of the wall-less city of Jerusalem. He goes before the king in a do-or-die moment, risking everything. The end result is a legacy that lives on to this day, almost 2,500 years later.

Just like Nehemiah, God has a plan and purpose for your life. Don't miss out on living your dash to the fullest because you were too cautious. Be willing to step out in faith and take a risk for God. How tragic to arrive at the end of your life, look in the rearview mirror and ask, "What if?" God is ready to do the impossible and he is ready to do it through you, if you are willing to take the risk.

We began this journey with the challenging words from Winston Churchill. Read his words again and see if you now believe them to be true in your life. *"There comes a special moment in everyone's life, a moment for which that person was born. That special opportunity, when he seizes it, will fulfill his mission - a mission for which he is uniquely qualified. In that moment, he finds greatness. It is his finest hour."*

There is without a doubt a mission God has for you to accomplish between today and your funeral. This is your dash, your life purpose. Whatever you do, don't miss it. Find out what God has planned for the remainder of your dash and do it.

When you get to the end of the journey, you may be bloody and bruised, worn out and used up. But if you listen carefully, you will be able to hear the voice of the One who lived his dash for your salvation say, *"Well done, good and faithful servant. You lived your dash on earth well. Now let's begin a new dash, a dash with fresh challenges and exciting adventures, a dash that will last forever, a dash you will live to the glory of God!"*

1. Eric Bell, Men of Mathematics (Simon and Schuster, New York, NY, 1937), page 375.

2. Rick Warren, *The Purpose Driven Church* (Zondervan Publishing House, Grand Rapids, Michigan, 1995).

3. Edgar A. Guest, "Somebody Said That It Couldn't Be Done" (www.poetryfoundation.org)

4. John Wesley, "Wesley Rejected" (www.sermonindex.net).

5. Edmund Fuller, 2500 Anecdotes for All Occasions (Avenel Books, Crown Publisher, Inc., New York, NY, 1980), page 72.

6. Quoted in Charles Swindoll, Hand Me Another Brick (Thomas Nelson, Nashville, Tennessee, 2006), pages 76-77.

7. Craig Brian Larson, Illustrations for Preaching and Teaching (Baker Books, Grand Rapids, Michigan, 1993), page 178.

8. Michael P. Green, Illustrations for Biblical Preaching (Baker Book House, Grand Rapids, Michigan, 1993), pages 71-72

9. Ibid, page 264.

10. Ted Engstrom, The Pursuit of Excellence (The Zondervan Corporation, Grand Rapids, Michigan, 1982).

11. H. Jackson Brown, Life's Little Instruction Book (Thomas Nelson, Nashville, Tennessee, 2012).

12. Michael P. Green, Illustrations for Biblical Preaching (Baker Book House, Grand Rapids, Michigan, 1993), pages 29-30.

13. Craig Brian Larson, Illustrations for Preaching and Teaching (Baker Books, Grand Rapids, Michigan, 1993), page 276.

14. Eugene H. Peterson, A Long Obedience in the Same Direction (InterVarsity Press, Downers Grove, Illinois, 1980).

15. Abraham Lincoln, "Proclamation for a National Day of Fasting, Humiliation and Prayer" (www.abrahamlincolnonline.org).

16. Craig Brian Larson, Illustrations for Preaching and Teaching (Baker Books, Grand Rapids, Michigan, 1993), page 74.

17. David Kinnaman, UnChristian (Baker Books, Grand Rapids, Michigan, 2007).

18. "Cautious Man" is quoted in John C. Maxwell, Developing the Leader Within You (Nelson Business, Nashville, Tennessee, 1993), page 191.

19. Anthony Campolo, Who Switched the Price Tags (Word Books, Waco, Texas, 1986), page 28.

DISCOVER THE LIFE-CHANGING EXPERIENCE OF TAKING THE LIVING YOUR DASH JOURNEY WITH A GROUP OF FRIENDS.

The *Living Your Dash* Small Group Curriculum is a six-part series produced by LifeTogether Ministries. It includes six small group DVD sessions taught by Rick Hale and a full-color study guide. This series also includes video training materials for small group leaders and hosts, and six powerful testimonies that drive home the message of each session.

lifetogether

DEEPEN YOUR SMALL GROUP'S
BIBLICAL UNDERSTANDING

Study sessions on DVDs with Small Group Questions following each session
and in-depth Bible Studies included on each DVD as PDF files.

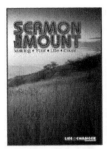

Sermon on the Mount:
Making Your Life Count

11 sessions on 4 DVDs

Party Frosting:
How to Enjoy the Rest of Your Life

A 9-Session study on the book of Paul's letters
to the Philippians on 3 DVDs. Explore topics
such as How to Treat People, Make A Difference
In Your World, and Making Peace With God.

Living Your Dash:
How to Find and Fulfill Your Life Purpose

A 9-Session study on 3 DVDs on the Book
of Nehemiah with topics such as how to Catch
God's Vision for your Life, How to Confirm Your
Life Mission, and Overcoming External Opposition.

We're working hard to enhance what we're offering to
help you study God's Word – the Bible – even more.
So we've created the Life Changer Podcast. This is a 30
minute format that will be great for your workouts, walks,
or other venues when you need a 30-minute pick-me-up.
We're also developing our iTunes channel so you and
your friends will be able to subscribe and receive each
new podcast weekly.

FOR THE LATEST INFORMATION ON INDIVIDUAL PRODUCTS, RELEASE DATES, AND FUTURE PROJECTS, VISIT
http://lifechangerstudies.com
Sign up and receive free updates!

ABOUT THE AUTHOR

Rick Hale is the Senior Pastor of Grace Community Church, an interdenominational church with a vision of helping people discover God's purpose for their lives. He has been a pastor since 1977, serving in various leadership positions. He is also involved with Community Bible Study where he is the local Teaching Director. In addition, he serves as the National Director of Conference Development for Community Bible Study and is a regular speaker at the organization's National Leadership Conference where his messages impact the lives of thousands of people. In 1980, he began a Thursday Noontime Bible Study which has become a mainstay in the community, deepening the faith of business leaders, retirees, and lunch-hour attendees for more than 30 years. He was educated at Abilene Christian University where he earned both Bachelor's and Master's degrees in Ministry. He is married to his wife Mary. They have two grown children.

Made in the USA
San Bernardino, CA
08 March 2016